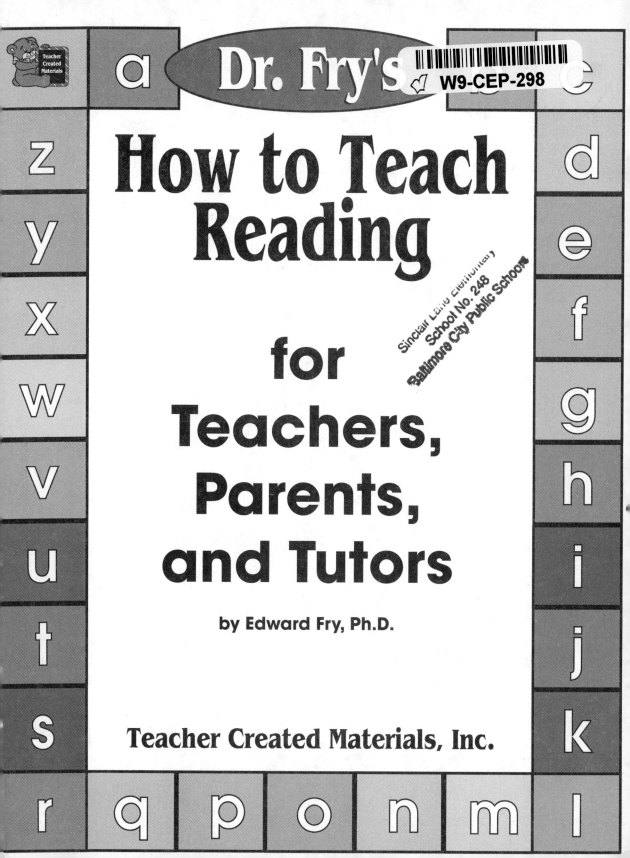

Dr. Fry's

W9-CEP-298

How to Teach Reading

for Teachers, Parents, and Tutors

by Edward Fry, Ph.D.

Teacher Created Materials, Inc.

How to Teach Reading
for
Teachers,
Parents,
and Tutors

Fourth Edition

by Edward Fry, Ph.D

Teacher Created Materials, Inc.
6421 Industry Way
Westminster, CA 92683
www.teachercreated.com

ISBN-1-57690-760-0

©*1995, Edward Fry, Ph.D.*
Laguna Beach Educational Books

©*1999, Revised by Teacher Created Materials, Inc.*

Reprinted, 2004
Made in U.S.A.

Table of Contents

Preface 6

Overview: How to Teach Reading 7
    Step 1: Determine the Student's Reading Ability 9
    Step 2: Select the Right Material for the Student to Read. 10
    Step 3: Have the Student Read Aloud and Silently
            with Comprehension 11
    Step 4: Teach Vocabulary. 12
    Step 5: Develop Phonics Skills 14
    Step 6: Writing, Speaking, Listening 15
    Trade Secrets. 16
           Success, Love, Discipline, Interest, Rewards, Fluency

Step 1: Determine the Student's Reading Ability. 20
    Purpose of the Oral Reading Test. 21
        Independent Reading Level, Instructional Reading Level,
        Frustration Reading Level

Step 2: Select the Right Material for the Student to Read 22
    Matching. 22
    Informal Matching 23
    Readability Graph. 24
    Interest Inventory 25
    Lists of Reading Material. 25
    Basal Readers 26
    Children's Literature. 26
    Special and Unconventional Reading Materials. 27
    Jokes 28
    Useful Sign Words 29
    Reading Numbers 29

Table of Contents *(cont.)*

Step 3: Have the Student Read Aloud and Silently
with Comprehension. 30
  Oral Reading and Fluency 30
  Variety in Subject Matter 31
  Variety in Length of Reading Selection 32
  Variety in Types of Questions. 34
  Variety in Difficulty of Level of Material 37
  Variety in Response 38
  Standardized Silent Reading Tests 40
  Silent Reading Comprehension Tests. 41
  Idiomatic Expressions. 42
  Songs. 43
  Reading Ideas 43

Step 4: Teach Vocabulary 44
  Testing the Instant Words 45
  Teaching the Instant Words. 46
      Easy Reading Practice, Flash Cards, Bingo Game,
      Pairs Game, Concentration Game, Spelling, Picture Nouns
  Vocabulary Building 56
      Pay Attention, Direct Instruction, Prefixes and Roots,
      Use New Words, Homophones

Step 5: Develop Phonics Skills 59
  Place of Teaching Phonics 59
  Learning the Alphabet. 60
  Writing the Alphabet. 60
  Phoneme Awareness 61
  Phonics Instruction 63
  Diagnosing Phonics Skills 64
  Methods of Teaching Phonics. 64
      Phonics Charts, Bingo, Spelling, Phonograms
  Phonics Warning. 68

Table of Contents *(cont.)*

Step 6: Writing, Speaking, Listening 69
   Language Experience Approach 70
   Story Starters 71
   Experience Charts 72
   Student-written Stories 73
   Handwriting 74
   Expository Writing 76
   Speaking 76
   Listening 77

Conclusion 79
   Ideas for Teaching Reading 79
   Sample Reading Lessons 81
   The Last Word 81

Appendix 82
   Oral Reading Test 82
   Interest Inventory for Children 92
   Interest Inventory for Adults 93
   Grade-Level Book Lists 94
   Silent Reading Comprehension Tests 96
   600 Instant Words 108
   Instant Words Test 114
   100 Picture Nouns 116
   Prefixes 118
   Greek Roots 120
   Latin Roots 121
   Homophones 123
   Important Signs 124
   Phonics Charts 125
   Phonograms 134
   Phonics Survey Test 138
   Story Starters List 140
   Handwriting Charts 141

Index 142

Preface

The first draft of this manual was developed at the Graduate School of Education at Rutgers University for a group of Peace Corps volunteers in training on campus. Their schedules were so crowded that little time was allotted for lectures on "How to Teach Reading," so I thought it best to give them something to carry into the field when needed.

I later discovered that there were many people who wanted to know how to teach reading and who didn't want to take a full university course or even read a thick teacher's textbook. So I rewrote the first draft into this little manual.

This book has been used by thousands of parents, adult literacy tutors, volunteers in programs for the disadvantaged, teachers' aides, and even classroom teachers who want a rapid overview of some proven methods of teaching reading. It has also been used by college students in laboratory and clinic-type teacher training courses.

This current revision is necessary because of some changes in the reading field. These changes include more emphasis on writing, fluency, and phonemic awareness. This new manual also has longer lists of phonic words, high-frequency words, and lists of reading materials. But basically, the six steps given in this manual have stood the test of time, and I am pleased to say they have helped many thousands of students read better.

Edward Fry, Ph.D.
245 Grandview Street
Laguna Beach, CA 92651

Overview: How to Teach Reading

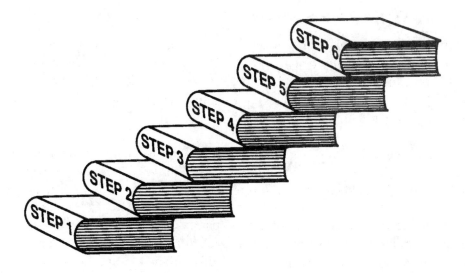

How do you teach a child or an adult to read?

This is an easy question and a difficult question. I can tell you in a sentence. I can tell you in a paragraph. I can tell you in a chapter. I can tell you in a whole book. And there would still be much more to be said.

But just to make my opening statement true, here is a one-sentence description of how you teach a student to read.

"You teach a student to read by helping him or her to learn the relationships between the printed words and their meanings."

You might say that that is not much of an explanation, and you are correct. But this explanation states a very fundamental concept underlying most reading instruction.

Now let's try a one-paragraph answer to the opening question.

"The teaching of reading usually begins by presenting the student with a story that has simple vocabulary arranged in short, easy sentences in a book or on a chart. The student is given help and is encouraged to practice reading these aloud

and silently. More words are added to the reading material, and the sentences and stories get longer. Phonics and phonemic awareness skills are taught. This means teaching the relationships between letters and sounds. Comprehension skills are usually taught by having the student read silently and answer various types of questions. The student learns to read common words, like the Instant Words and meaningful words like names, both in stories and isolation. Writing is introduced; the student starts to write and read his own stories. The printed stories, student-written stories, phonics lessons, and comprehension drills gradually increase in difficulty as the student gains in ability. Usually quite a bit of reading practice and frequent review lessons are necessary."

I hope that you found the one-paragraph explanation of teaching reading more satisfactory. But I will admit that it still does not give you too much insight into the reading process or specific methods of teaching reading. So I will now give you the one-chapter explanation, which will be followed by some additional information.

This book is written from the standpoint of a teacher, tutor, or parent working with an individual student. Certainly, many of the methods discussed here apply to small groups or even classrooms, but to understand the reading process, we must consider what happens to "a student," not some vague thing called "a group."

The methods in this book are suitable for beginning readers and remedial readers of any age from five or six years through adults. The reading skills needed are the same for any beginning reader—simple reading material, learning common words, phonics, and comprehension. The main difference between young children, teenagers, and adults is in the content of the stories. For example, young children might like to read fairy tales, while older readers may prefer sports stories or mysteries.

Step 1: Determine the Student's Reading Ability

The first thing to determine is the present reading level of the student. Do not go by size, age, how many years the student has been in school, or other factors which have only a general correlation with reading skills. Find out for yourself as closely as possible what level of material the student can successfully read. This can be quickly and easily done by using the Oral Reading Test (pages 82–91) and other informal methods which are discussed in the Step 1 chapter beginning on page 20.

Below is an example from the Oral Reading Test.

Sample Oral Reading Test

Easy First-Grade Difficulty

Look at the dog.

It is big.

It can run.

Run, dog, run away.

Fifth-Grade Difficulty

High in the hills they came to a wide ledge where trees grew among the rocks. Grass grew in patches, and the ground was covered with bits of wood from trees blown over a long time ago and dried by the sun. Down in the valley it was already beginning to get dark.

Step 2: Select the Right Material for the Student to Read

After you have determined your student's reading ability level, select or create reading material of the appropriate level. You can determine the grade level for any story you think he or she should read by simply using the Readability Graph (page 24). In other words, what this first step is telling you to do is to **match the reading ability of the student with the difficulty level of the material**. You really need to do a careful and accurate job of matching because the further you miss the match, the more difficult your teaching job will be, and the closer the match, the easier it will be.

Another useful way of determining whether the reading material is at the proper level for the student is simply to ask him or her to read a bit of it aloud. If he or she makes two or more mistakes for every 20 words, the material is too difficult. If the student makes almost no mistakes for every 20 words, he or she should be able to read it silently with reasonable ease. If about one mistake is made for every 20 words, then this material is at his or her instructional level. Material at the instructional level can be used in oral reading lessons or for silent reading when someone is close at hand to help him or her with difficult words. Do not use material that is too difficult. It blocks learning, frustrates the student, and makes your job harder. Do not use the Oral Reading Test for instruction; use other reading material.

Judging Book Difficulty
by Students' Oral Reading Errors

Independent Reading Level = No mistakes in 20 words
Good for silent reading practice and recreational reading

Instructional Level = About one mistake in 20 words
Good for reading with teacher's or friend's help

Frustration Level = Two or more mistakes in 20 words
Don't use. Get an easier book.

It is, of course, very desirable to have interesting reading material. Students like to read about fancy automobiles, sports, adventure, interesting careers, romance (if older), mysteries, and stories about their heritage. They also like to read notes and stories you write for them, their own stories, and classmates' stories.

Very beginning reading lessons are frequently done using teacher-written words, phrases, or very short stories. They can be printed on a piece of paper, the chalkboard or white board, a chart or large piece of paper, or on cards to be used in a pocket chart. The oral reading tests on pages 85-87 can give you an idea of how difficult your writing should be, but please do not use the oral test paragraphs for instruction; save them for measuring progress (testing).

Step 3: Have the Student Read Aloud and Silently with Comprehension

After you have found the student's reading ability level and matched it with the correct reading material, what do you do? Have him or her read it aloud, helping as often as necessary. You also must have the student practice reading silently, helping if needed. This can be done alone or in small groups. You can have the student reread the same short passage orally several times to improve "fluency" with each rereading.

Keep these practice lessons short so the student does not become bored or frustrated. Schedule them regularly and frequently. For student interest, reading material can be presented on charts, games, pamphlets, or cards; it doesn't really matter how it is presented as long as it is at the right level and your student is comprehending it.

There is no point in having your student read aloud or silently if he or she doesn't understand what is being reading. The purpose of reading is to receive the author's ideas.

With beginning readers, teaching comprehension is usually not too difficult. Their speaking and listening vocabularies are so far above their reading vocabulary that comprehension takes place almost automatically when you show them the relationship between written and spoken language.

However, within just a few years of reading development, comprehension becomes a major concern and usually must be taught specifically. Written or oral questions following silent or oral reading is the usual method.

Children simply can't learn to read with comprehension unless they practice. It takes practice to learn to read orally and silently and to comprehend. Do not, however, make this an excuse for giving a lot of boring drills.

You can use variety to keep the reading lesson moving. Go from oral reading to silent reading comprehension drills to the methods suggested in Steps 4 and 5 for teaching the Instant Words (a basic sight-word list) and phonics. I often tell teachers to have three or four different kinds of reading activities per hour. Schedule regular lesson periods and stick to them.

Of course, one of the best methods of practice is simply to get a book that the student is interested in and let him or her read. Usually, to get a student to read silently for a long period of time, you must give him or her a book that is a little on the easy side. For silent pleasure reading, help the student select a book that is easier than you would use for instruction. Your encouragement, visits to the library, assignment of oral or written book reports, and so on, will encourage your student to read on his or her own.

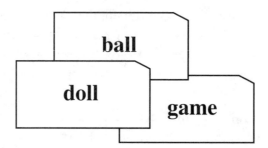

Step 4: Teach Vocabulary

For children and all learners, things to be taught are usually presented in graded order of difficulty, with easiest things first. Much work has been done in the reading field to determine the proper vocabulary and its order of presentation for the teaching of reading. This is the strong point of most major traditional series of reading texts. They begin with very few words in the first little book and gradually increase the vocabulary load. This vocabulary load increase can be seen on the last few pages of most children's reading texts. So, teachers using a traditional basic reading series have a built-in graduated vocabulary. Many modern teachers now use children's literature books and predictable books for beginners. These children's literature books do not have carefully controlled vocabulary or vocabulary lists. See the Step 4 chapter beginning on page 44 for how to teach vocabulary.

However, in remedial reading, individualized reading, and literature-based reading programs, it is a good idea to supplement and cross-check vocabulary development and have some systematic list of new words to be taught. One such list is the Instant Words, the most common words in the English language. They are arranged in order of frequency of occurrence in reading material and in children's writing.

Instant Words

Below are the 10 most frequently used words in the English language. At least one of them appears in almost every sentence. A person who cannot read these, cannot read much.

the	in
of	is
and	you
a	that
to	it

A list of 600 Instant Words is on pages 108–113. See the Step 4 chapter for how to teach them.

A student should learn to recognize them instantly in order to have ease in reading because they occur so very often. The first 100 words make up almost one-half of all reading material.

You can use the Instant Words Test on pages 114 and 115 to determine which group of Instant Words to start teaching. Several methods for teaching the Instant Words are in the Step 4 chapter, beginning on page 44.

Step 5: Develop Phonics Skills

Basically, we have a phonetic language. This means that letters and some letter groups have regular speech sounds. There are plenty of exceptions, but every good reader should know at least the basic phonics principles. Phonics skills are a tremendous help to any student learning how to read. They are also helpful in spelling lessons and in using the dictionary.

There are phonics charts with carefully chosen example words in the Appendix on pages 125-133, which will help you teach all the major phonetic rules. The Phonics Survey Test on pages 138 and 139 will help you quickly find which main phonics skills the student knows or does not know.

Exactly when to begin teaching phonics is an emotionally loaded question. Research results are inconclusive. Personally, I think phonics instruction should begin in kindergarten with alphabet activities like playing with letters, coloring them, and mentioning their sounds and with phoneme awareness activities such as poems that emphasize different speech sounds. Regular phonics lessons should continue at the first-grade level and be completed by the third-grade level with some repetition, remedial lessons, and fine points taught even later.

Phonics is now taught as part of a spelling program in many schools. It doesn't make any difference whether you call it reading or spelling as long as the student learns the relationships between the letters and their sounds. In phonics, as in everything else, you start with what the student knows and then you test, teach, test again, and teach some more.

Phonics Examples

The basic idea in phonics instruction is to help the reader learn the connection between letters or letter groups and their speech sounds.

Similar Beginning Letter /k/	Similar Vowel Sound /i/	Phonograms /-it/
kind	five	bit
keep	ride	sit
kill	time	hit
key	like	fit

Step 6: Writing, Speaking, Listening

In the past, many schools and reading teachers separated reading and writing into two separate lessons. Now it is common to have both reading and writing as part of the same lesson, at least some of the time. Literacy is defined as the ability to both read and write.

You can easily combine some of your lessons to include reading and writing. The Step 6 chapter beginning on page 69, not only gives suggestions on writing fundamentals like handwriting and spelling, but it will also encourage you to have children write some of their own reading material. Student-written stories can be a real creative outlet. Teachers can also write stories and develop experience charts that are interesting for their students to read because they are about topics of the students' own special interests.

Students of any age immediately see the usefulness of learning to write. There are many times in school, at work, and at home when writing is a valuable skill. There is also evidence that language uses—reading, writing, speaking, and listening—are interrelated. A good teacher helps to develop them all. The Step 6 chapter also gives some suggestions on improving speaking and listening.

Trade Secrets

The following are a few tricks of the teaching trade that we learned in the Reading Center at Rutgers University. Though they apply especially to children having problems learning to read (remedial readers), they also apply to average students and adult learners in regular classrooms.

Success

Nothing motivates like success. In the Reading Center we say that a student must be successful with every lesson. If he or she is not, then we, the tutors, have given the wrong lesson or have taught in the wrong manner. We first seek a level where the student can be successful. If he or she can't read a new sentence in an easy book, we teach just one word and say, "That's great! We are really getting somewhere now. Let's see if we can learn two new words today." By building little successes upon little successes, you can soon change a sullen, reluctant reader into an eager learner.

Love

Students and adults who cannot read are rejected in many ways every day in school and in the world. They are set aside. They are different. They are failures. Not only have teachers failed to teach them, but teachers and society also constantly remind them of their problem just by giving the usual reading assignments in social studies or arithmetic or by having written directions and newspapers around.

The successful reading teacher should remedy as many aspects of this situation as possible. If love is too strong a word, let's say that the teacher must care about the student and must use words and deeds to demonstrate that he or she cares.

Discipline

Just as love suggests a certain warmth and allowance for personality differences, so discipline provides some structure for the teaching situation. It's important that a student get to lessons on time, have a minimum of absences, pay attention during lessons, and not be disruptive. Occasionally after a few weeks of instruction, it is necessary to offer some students a choice to either stop their reading lessons or settle down. It is highly unlikely the student would decide to stop, but let him or her stop if that is what is wanted. You can lead a horse to water, but you can't make it drink. The decision to learn must be the student's and not the parent's or the teacher's.

Interest

Most students are pretty poor actors when it comes to feigning interest. Learn to read the signs of lack of interest: losing the place in oral reading, daydreaming, fiddling with irrelevant objects, and so on. Discipline won't make boring lessons good lessons. The teacher must be skillful enough to present lessons that are easy enough to provide success but difficult enough to provide challenge and growth.

Try to find reading materials that have a natural interest for the student. Turn some of your drills into competitive games, again keeping in mind that each student must experience some success. Students like to read about baseball, skin diving, mysteries, and so on, not stories about neat little children in short pants pulling wagons. Adults might find a lot of interest in reading want ads about good paying jobs or driver's license manuals.

Rewards

Most people have their behavior modified by rewards. How long would most people go to work if they were not paid? Even when we do things without being paid, we get some kinds of reward: the satisfaction of helping others, fun, companionship, or interest in doing something new. Sometimes the reward can be delayed—most people go to school so that eventually they will earn more money. But all of us, especially children, like to have some immediate rewards. Hence, the teacher should use a wide variety of rewards. Here are a few suggestions:

- Praise a student at least once every lesson for something done well.

- Keep a progress chart of new words learned.

- Give gold stars or little trinkets for lessons completed or done especially well.

- See that the student has a chance to use his or her new skills in a meaningful situation.

- Have games that even slower students can win occasionally.

Fluency

Good readers and good writers seem to do it almost effortlessly. They make it look easy. And how did they achieve that? The answer is by much practice. In fact, the experts in any skill—from playing tennis to playing the violin— have to practice often. It is, of course, quite possible to have some natural ability in any skill, including reading and writing, but most people need practice to develop a skill, and even those with natural ability get better with practice.

You need to develop fluency, which can be defined as effortless reading with good comprehension, in your students. One way to do this is to give a lot of practice on an easy level before progressing to the next level of difficulty. You can teach fluency directly by having the student read a short story or passage on any subject three or four times, trying to improve each time. It is helpful if you model oral reading by reading the passage aloud, paying attention to pauses indicated by commas or other punctuation and also stressing important words to get a better "sentence tune." Make sure the student has not only mastered a story (reads it without errors and has good comprehension) but also has much additional practice on the story before progressing. Progressing too fast causes frustration, failure to learn, and quitting (dropping out of school or stopping lessons).

Now you've had a one-sentence answer, a one-paragraph answer, and a one-chapter answer to this question: How do you teach a child or an adult to read?

With this information and the more detailed information given in the rest of this book, you can help almost any student learn to read better.

Good luck!

Step 1: Determine the Student's Reading Ability

Here you are, getting ready for your first session of teaching reading. What is your first step? It is to find out the present reading level of the student.

There are very few students in school or adults in the civilized world who read nothing. Almost everybody has some reading ability. The questions is, "How much?"

Don't waste your time complaining that somebody else or some system should have taught your student how to read before this. Just find out how much your student can read right now, then get to work with lessons. Your student will thank you for the rest of his or her life when you are successful. Complaining never taught anybody anything.

How do you determine a student's present reading level? You test him or her with the Oral Reading Test (pages 82-91). Carefully read the following material that explains exactly how to use the Oral Reading Test. Then proceed with your first testing session. There are other important methods of measuring the student's reading skills, but these will be discussed later.

Purpose of the Oral Reading Test

The purpose of this test is to aid instruction by determining the Independent Reading Level and the Instructional Reading Level of a child or an adult by having him or her read aloud several paragraphs.

Independent Reading Level

The Independent Reading Level is that difficulty level of reading material at which the student can read with relative ease and independence; in other words, the student can read with little or no help from the instructor. The student should be able to pronounce nearly all the words at this level. You can give your student reading material at this level for pleasure, practice, and sustained silent reading.

Instructional Reading Level

The Instructional Reading Level is that difficulty level of reading material at which reading instruction is most effective. The student should know most of the words, not all. Use this level for instruction, such as oral reading or silent reading, when you are around to help him or her with difficult words.

Frustration Reading Level

If reading instruction is given with material at too hard a level (that is, with too many unknown words), then the student's progress is not as rapid and symptoms of nervousness and dislike of reading may occur. Most of the time you should avoid getting your student reading material at his or her frustration level.

The Oral Test also asks you to use your judgment as to the student's fluency, which involves such factors as speed and meaningful intonation of sentences. Fluency will give you some insight into the student's ability to understand what is being read. Now turn to the test section at the end of this manual, glance over the Oral Reading Test (see pages 82-91), and administer the test to your student.

Step 2: Select the Right Material for the Student to Read

Now you know how well your student can read. Because you have used the Oral Reading Test, you know his or her Independent Reading Level and Instructional Reading Level. Sometimes they are the same, but in any event, avoid the Frustration Reading Level (see pages 10 and 21).

Your next step is to find reading materials at the right level for the student. With the Readability Graph (page 24), you can find the reading level of any book or story. From the lists of reading materials in the Appendix (pages 94 and 95), you can find descriptions of instructional materials written at specific reading levels.

Matching

Matching and selecting the right reading material for your student is one of your most important jobs. If you give a student material that is too hard, the student may become frustrated and stop reading, or his or her comprehension of the material will be poor. Even if the student does struggle through it, it will take an excessive amount of time. On the other hand, if the student is given material that is too easy, he or she may find it "babyish" and become bored and stop reading.

The basic interest in the subject itself is, of course, an important factor. With very high interest, the student may work through more difficult material. But with only a normal amount of interest in the subject matter, the student will stop reading if the material is too difficult. And most teachers agree that it is very important for students to read widely and frequently.

On the next page is a graph that will tell you the approximate difficulty level of any reading material. Use it in judging the grade level of reading material for your student. Try to match his or her reading ability (grade level obtained from the Oral Reading Test) with the grade level of the material. Remember, it is better to have the material a little too easy than a little too hard for reading instruction and especially for silent reading.

Informal Matching

If you don't want to use the Oral Reading Test and Readability Graph as aids in selecting material, you can match your student to a book by using the one-error-in-20-words method shown in the box on page 10.

Leveling

In addition to the Readability Graph, there are additional ways to judge the difficulty of a text. These factors are more useful at beginning reading levels (grades 1-3), but most apply to any reading material.

- **Length**—Beginning readers can be overwhelmed by too many words on a page or too many pages in a book or story. Hence, keep it short and simple at first.
- **Illustrations**—Good illustrations add interest and aid comprehension.
- **Content**—Familiarity with the story setting, characters, or content make for easier reading. Avoid complicated plots in the beginning.
- **Language Structure**—Some writing is easier for the reader, such as short declarative sentences, interesting dialog, predictability, and repetition of difficult words or phrases.
- **Format**—The print type size and page layout can make text look easy or hard.

If not using a readability formula, then you must take two main factors into account when judging the difficulty of written material. These are:

1. **Vocabulary difficulty:** Unfamiliar words make reading harder.
2. **Sentence length:** The average sentence should be short for beginning readers.

Readability Graph

Average number of syllables per 100 words

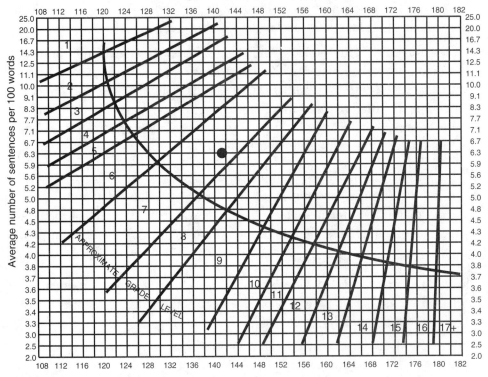

Directions: To determine the grade level of reading material, randomly select three 100-word passages from a book or an article. Count proper nouns, numerals, and initials as words. Count each symbol (letter or number) as a syllable. For instance, "1945" has four numbers and should be counted as four syllables; "IRA" has three letters and should be counted as three syllables.

Determine the average number of syllables and average number of sentences per 100 words (see the example below). If a wide variability is observed, the book has uneven readability.

Then plot the average syllables and sentences on the Readability Graph above. The numbers between each set of boldface lines indicate the approximate grade level of the reading material. The curved, boldface line shows the norm. If the averages fall outside the lines, grade-level scores are invalid and other reading material should be selected.

Example:

	Syllables	Sentences
First 100 Words	124	6.6
Second 100 Words	141	5.5
Third 100 Words	<u>158</u>	<u>6.8</u>
Average	141	6.3

Readability = 7th Grade (See the sample dot marked on the graph above.)

Interest Inventory

Most teachers find an interest inventory a good way of finding out about some of the students' interests. You will find an Interest Inventory for children and one for adults. The inventories can be used in part or in whole so that you can know more about your students' interests. If a student is deficient in writing skills, fill it out for him or her in an interview situation, or just use the Interest Inventory as a suggestion list and ask the student some of the items. Take a moment right now and look at these Interest Inventories on pages 92 and 93 in the Appendix.

Filling out the inventory should be a pleasant experience, not a chore. Tell the student that every question doesn't have to be answered. Don't penalize for spelling, but give help if needed. Most of these answers could use more space, so suggest the back of the sheet if needed.

In addition, almost any of the items on the inventory could be the suggested topic for a theme. Many of the individual items (questions) can be used orally to start a conversation with your student. They show the student that you are interested in him or her. Finally, use the answers to the inventory items in selecting stories and reading materials for lessons.

Lists of Reading Materials

In the Appendix, you will find a list of books sorted by grade level. These are books frequently used in schools, but they can also be purchased directly from the publisher. Most public libraries have several of these books. You can use the stories in these books for oral reading, or you can use them for silent reading. Teachers, school librarians, and public librarians can help you select interesting and easy reading material for your student.

These books are graded by well-known educators (Fountas, Pinnell, Gunning) to help you match your students' reading abilities (Oral Reading Test score) with the proper difficulty of the book. Take a moment right now to look over the book lists on pages 94 and 95 in the Appendix.

Basal Readers

Children in school frequently learn to read from a set of books called a "basal reading" series. These series have stories and exercises for each grade level, usually one through six. These books can be used to teach reading to either children or adults, but one serious problem in using them is that they are often childish for older students. For some students, basal readers represent the kind of material that they have failed with and, hence, they have bad associations. So you must decide whether or not you want to use some books from a basal series or not. Basal readers can be used in part; in other words, you can just select a few stories in any book for use by your student. Sometimes public schools will lend or give you old copies of basal readers. Just ask the principal of a nearby school. Also, many public libraries have copies of basal readers that they lend out free. One advantage of basal readers is that they are already graded (first-grade difficulty, second grade, etc.).

Children's Literature

Children's literature books are the common children's storybooks found in bookstores and libraries. Some are "classics" like *Little Red Riding Hood,* and some were just written last year and may become classics. But be careful of this distinction:

> Some books are meant to be read *to* children.
> Some books are meant to be read *by* children.

For example, Dr. Seuss's *Cat in the Hat* is meant to be read *by* children because it uses simple words, repetition, and easier sentence construction, and is thus suitable for first-grade level. But Dr. Seuss's *How the Grinch Stole Christmas* is meant to be read *to* children, because it is at the Frustrating Reading Level for most first graders.

There is a special type of children's trade books called "predictable" books or stories. These have a lot of repetition and are useful in teaching reading to children or even adults of any age. For an example of a predictable (repetitious) story, see the sample children's story "Busy, Busy Day" on page 148 in the Appendix. For older children or adults, the song "She'll Be Comin' Round the Mountain" on page 43 has a lot of repetition and can be used for reading instruction and fun.

Special and Unconventional Reading Materials

Good teachers and tutors often strive to make reading lessons more interesting by bringing to class special reading materials. Look over the list below for some ideas for your students.

- **Driver's license examination booklet**
- **Articles from a newspaper** on the World Series, a local crime, a fashion tip, job want ads, a scientific discovery, a human interest story
- **Directions** for assembling a toy or an appliance
- **Jokes**
- **Lyrics** for a popular song
- **Short poems** to be memorized
- **Signs** and warnings
- **Local maps** and **bus schedules**
- **Post office forms**
- **Student newspapers** like *My Weekly Reader, Time for Kids,* or *Scholastic*; used copies of these are sometimes given away by public schools.

Jokes

Joke books or joke columns in newspapers or magazines make entertaining reading for both children and adults. Because the content is amusing, students actually enjoy reading. Here are a few samples.

Books never written:
How to Do Gymnastics by Leo Tard
Different Types of Sickness by Ty Foid
Exercise Made Easy by Jim E. Quipment
Fast Cars by Otto Mobile

What do you call...
a cow with no legs? (*ground beef*)
1000 rabbits moving backwards? (*a receding hare line*)
a box lunch? (*a square meal*)
a skeleton that rings bells? (*a dead ringer*)

What is the laziest mountain in the world?
Mount Ever Rest

How does a car feel after a long trip?
Exhausted

Why did Humpty Dumpty have a great fall?
To make up for a crummy summer

What do you get when you put four ducks in a small box?
A box full of quackers

What do you get when you cross...
a pig and a pine tree? (*a pork-u-pine*)
an owl and a goat? (*a hootenanny*)

Useful Sign Words

Words on signs are important. Everyone needs to learn how to read these words whether for safety, to get to places, or to avoid embarrassment. Below are some useful sign words. An additional list of Important Signs is on page 124 in the Appendix. You can also make your own list of common, useful signs and words.

Ask students to bring in a list of sign words seen in their neighborhood or in stores. It is also helpful to have a list of label words like "milk" or "soup." Perhaps the teacher and the student could bring in one sign or label word each lesson day.

Airport	**Gentlemen**	**Stop**
Bus	**Ladies**	**Taxi**
Danger	**Men**	**Walk**
Exit	**School Zone**	**Women**

Reading Numbers

Students learning to read often do not know how to read numbers, particularly large numbers. Start out teaching some low numbers like "22," "96," "45," and work your way up to "124," "541," or "8,799."

Step 3: Have the Student Read Aloud and Silently with Comprehension

You have taken two important steps.

1. You have found your student's reading level.
2. You have matched it with the right reading material.

Now what? Now you must get your student to read and read and read. The student should read orally with comprehension. He or she should read silently with comprehension and fluency.

Oral Reading and Fluency

Having the student read aloud is a time-honored method for teaching reading. It is not a bad method, but it is certainly limited and, in some schools and tutoring situations, vastly overused. Simply having the student read aloud is, at best, a good diagnostic tool. The teacher learns a lot about what the student knows about reading and word recognition. It is important to help the teacher to select the proper difficulty of reading material. Remember the one-error-in-20 words method shown in the box on page 10.

Most teachers use oral reading as a springboard for pointing out unknown words and also a bit of instant phonics instruction with unknown words (for example, asking the student, "What sound does this word begin with?")

However, a newer emphasis on oral reading aims at the teaching of "fluency." *Fluency* means reading at a reasonable speed without hesitations and with proper emphasis or intonation. Emphasis is part of "sentence tunes." For example, the voice is raised if the sentence is a question. Sometimes the emphasis is indicated by punctuation marks like a question mark (?), a period (.), an exclamation mark (!), or a comma (,). But more often, the student must provide the emphasis based on comprehension of the meaning or the meaning the student wishes to infer.

Try shifting the emphasis on different words in this sentence:

"I did not say you stole my red banana."

If you emphasize the "I," it infers that perhaps someone else said you stole the banana. If you emphasize "stole," perhaps you just borrowed it. Do the same with the other words in the sentence.

Not every sentence is subject to such radical shifts in meaning by stressing different words, but all sentences do have one or more tunes, which can emphasize the meaning.

To teach fluency, select a passage at the student's instructional level. For very young students, perhaps the passage will be one or two short sentences. Increase the passage length as the reader gets more advanced reading skills. After you have the passage selected, have the student reread the same passage several times to gain speed. Correct any word mispronunciations. Improve the sentence tune with each re-reading. The object of the fluency reading drill is not a high rate of speed, but an even, pleasing flow with proper emphasis-demonstration mastery and comprehension of the passage.

A good technique is to tell the student that he or she is a radio announcer and will be broadcasting the passage. Some teachers might like to use a tape recorder so that the student can hear himself or herself improving with each repeated reading. More perfected passages can also be used for a classroom performance. These can be short dramatic pieces, jokes, poems, newspaper articles, or other materials. Variety will add interest to your lessons and help to keep practice from becoming boring.

Variety in Subject Matter

The subject matter is one of the most obvious things that can be varied. It takes one approach to comprehend a set of directions on how to build a model airplane or how to bake a cake. It takes an entirely different approach to comprehend a story and still another approach for a history lesson.

All of these approaches involve reading, but you would want your student to read the history lesson more slowly and carefully than the story and the directions even more carefully. What the author intends you to get from a story is not the same as what the author intends you to get from a history lesson or from a set of directions. You should point this out to the student. And the best way to point it out is not by lecturing but by giving the student some simple questions following the reading.

Here are a few suggestions of different types of subject matter that you might select for comprehension drills and reading practice.

Subject Variety Suggestions

Adventure stories—jungles, space, mountain climbing, foreign travel

Biography—lives of heroes or heroines, famous people, minority leaders, movie stars

Sports—baseball, auto racing, football, basketball (Newspaper accounts of current sports events are sometimes especially useful with older students)

How to do it—get a job, repair a car, build a model, bake a cake, health and body building, beauty aids

Romance and family situations—overcoming personal problems

Strange and interesting—how people lived long ago, ancestors, causes of death, wars, floods, great inventions, animal stories, magic

---

Variety in Length of Reading Selection

The length of the reading selection should be varied. In the beginning, getting your student to read one word or one sentence is often a feat. But even after learning to read a whole paragraph, your student should sometimes focus on only one word or one sentence. As his or her ability advances, you will no doubt give comprehension drills based on reading a paragraph or several paragraphs. This is a standard technique. As soon as possible, the student should read a whole story and then a whole book. Some students take real pride in having accomplished the feat of reading a whole book.

You can see the amount of variety you can add to comprehension drills by focusing on these different lengths of material:

Length Variety Suggestions

A Word: Getting the meaning of one word is often called vocabulary building, but it is a kind of comprehension skill. Teachers should discuss and ask questions about one word sometimes. Also see Step 4: Teach Vocabulary.

A Phrase: Several words together often take on a meaning not contained in one word alone. The phrase "under the weather" doesn't have much to do with weather. See the list of idioms on page 42.

A Sentence: Sentences can be short and sweet with a simple noun-verb-object pattern, or they can be very complex with conditionals, subordinate clauses, and so on. Pick out some long and short sentences from the material you are using, discuss them, and ask comprehension questions about them.

Length Variety Suggestions *(cont.)*

A Paragraph: This is a traditional unit of teaching comprehension. It is good and should be used, but not exclusively. Be sure to use variety in the questions asked.

A Chapter or Story: In many books, groups of paragraphs form a larger unit. Teach your students to read larger units. Show that sometimes you have to see several paragraphs in relation to each other to get meaning. Ask questions that can only be answered by reading many paragraphs or the whole story.

A Book: Even younger students like long stories sometimes. Guide them into reading easy whole books, then slightly harder ones.

Variety in Types of Questions

The types of questions can be very important in teaching comprehension. The easiest type of question to ask is the "specific detail" question such as "What was the color of the boy's hair?" It is good to get the facts straight, but there are some more interesting types of questions that you can use. Avoid questions that can be answered "yes" or "no" or with a one-word answer.

Types of Questions

Time Sequence:

What happened first?

What happened next?

What happened after...?

When did the characters...?

Setting:

Where does this story take place: at home, in the park, in the city, in the country? (specific)

Where does this story take place: out West, in New York, in America, in Europe, in outer space? (general)

In what period of time does this story take place; in a morning, a day, a year?

In what period of history does this story take place: modern day, during Word War II, in the Middle Ages, in prehistoric times?

What do you know about that period from other things you have read?

What was the weather like? Did it have anything to do with how the characters felt or with what happened?

Summary:

Restate the paragraph or story in your own words.

Types of Questions *(cont.)*

NOTE: The questions below often require the student to do some creative interpreting since they may not be answered directly in the story.

Main Idea: What is this story (article) about?

What point is the writer making? What is the main idea of paragraph . . .? Is the main idea stated in the paragraph?

What is the main idea of the whole story (article)?

Why did the writer choose this title for the story?

Can you think of a better title?

Character Traits: What does the hero look like? What kind of person do you think he or she is? Why?

Is the hero happy? Honest? Why?

Conclusions: How do you think the writer feels about. . .? Why?

What can you conclude from this story about. . .? Why?

Which of the following is probably true. . .? Why?

When the hero said, ". . .," how do you think he or she felt? Why?

What might happen next? (if the story was to continue)

Types of Questions *(cont.)*

NOTE: Keep in mind that a conclusion must be supported by facts in the story. In response to "Why?" the student should support his or her answer by referring to the story.

5 W's + H Questions: Who? What? Where? When? Why? How?

Comparison: Is this better than the last story you read?

Which story was written first?

Was anything about the two heroes the same? Different?

What else do you know about people or events like this?

By using a variety of questions, you can keep the student interested and also cover a wide range of comprehension skills. Don't ask questions that require comprehension skills that are above the level of your student. Ask questions that the student can often answer successfully.

Variety in Difficulty of Level of Material

The difficulty level of the material should be varied. Of course, you want to give a lot of practice on easy material because it helps the reader feel successful, and this is very important. So first try out comprehension drills on easy material, then on slightly harder material. If the student experiences failure or frustration, return to the easy material for awhile.

Attempting to vary the difficulty level can add interest. Sometimes students will enjoy doing a comprehension drill or reading a book that is very simple for them, but sometimes they feel absolutely triumphant about mastering harder material.

Variety in Response

The type of response that you ask a student to make to a question is very important and can have some variety. Perhaps the easiest type of question requires some memory or "recall," as the psychologists like to call it. A question is asked, and the student gives an answer. The questions or directions may specify whether a **long answer** (sentence or several sentences) is required or a **short answer** (word or phrase) is required.

Another type of answer variation is between **written** and **oral** answers. Sometimes the teacher will want the student to answer with his or her pencil and sometimes by speaking. The same type of variation also applies to the kind of reading done; that is, the reading may be oral or silent. Thus, a teacher may have oral questions following silent reading one day and silently read questions and written responses following oral reading of the passage on the next day.

Multiple-choice questions are often used in commercially prepared comprehension drills. Not only is this type of question good for comprehension drills, but it is also frequently the kind of question used in testing the student's knowledge in a wide variety of situations. Hence, the student should have some practice in handling this type of question. Occasionally, students enjoy making up multiple-choice questions for each other on some reading material. A similar type of choice question, but limited to two choices, is the true/false type of question.

Cloze is another type of comprehension drill question. It is also sometimes called the sentence completion technique. To make cloze questions is very simple. Just knock out a word—any word—in a sentence and see if the student can fill it in. The simplest type of cloze drill is mechanical deletion, where you might just leave out every tenth word. More meaningful exercises might have more meaningful deletions, such as only subject matter words (noun, adjective, verb, or adverb). Do not delete more than every tenth word, or else the student will get a little frustrated with the task. Some students, particularly students for whom English is a second language, need drills on language usage. For these students, cloze techniques which knock out structure words (anything not a subject word) are very interesting as well as beneficial. For example, in making a structure word cloze drill, you might have a paragraph like this:

> **Rosa went to _____ store for her mother.**
>
> **"Are you the new girl?" asked the man _____ the store.**

The student's task is to fill in the missing words. Select passages that are on the easy-reading side for the student.

You can also get into some interesting discussions about the exact word versus the kind of word that can be put into the blank space.

Don't use this type of drill too much. It is excellent, but if overused it becomes boring. Stick to the main idea of this chapter: variety.

Student-generated questions are sometimes fun. Simply ask your student to make up his or her own questions for a paragraph or a story. The teacher then must answer the student's questions and discuss the answers. If you have two or more students, they can make up questions for each other. Be sure to reward the student making up the questions by much praise like, "That's a fine question; it really made me think." By praising just the good questions, you can get a better set of questions the next time you do this type of lesson.

Retelling the story is a simple but very effective comprehension lesson. Simply ask the student to retell the story in his or her own words after having read it silently. If the student cannot tell you the story, there is a good chance he or she has not understood it. If this happens, just ask the student to read the story again a little more carefully because you are going to ask him or her to tell you all about it. This will also give you the opportunity to teach comprehension by saying, "If there is any part that you do not understand, just ask me about it." Incidentally, the retelling can be either oral or written. If the student has sufficient writing skills, ask him or her to write a story version of the story in his or her own words. You can also help with his or her writing skills.

If the student is bilingual and you are bilingual (for example, if you both speak Spanish), ask the student to read the story in English but tell you about it in Spanish. This is an excellent comprehension check.

Response Variety Summary

1. Variety in answer length (for example: long, short)

2. Multiple choice or true/false

3. Cloze—filling in missing word(s)

4. Student makes up questions

5. Retelling or summarizing

Standardized Silent Reading Tests

Schools often give reading tests, and the scores are available to parents, teachers, and tutors. The names of some important reading achievement tests are California Reading Test, Stanford, SRA, Metropolitan, and Iowa.

It is important to know a little bit about silent reading tests. Formal or standardized tests tell you approximately what grade level of reading ability the student has achieved. These tests are another important measure (along with the oral tests) of the student's reading ability. They are useful for measuring progress over the period of a year or more, and they are useful in helping you select books and stories at the proper difficulty level.

Not every section of a standardized silent reading test is equally valuable. The most important part, or the part that you should pay the most careful attention to, is the part which measures paragraph comprehension. This section is sometimes called "Comprehension" or "Reading Interpretations." It consists of asking the student to read one or several paragraphs and then to answer one or more questions about what he or she has just read.

Silent Reading Comprehension Tests

You may wish to test your student's reading comprehension. It is not required, but it does give you some more information about your student's reading ability.

In the Appendix on pages 98-107 are two Silent Reading Comprehension Tests that you can use to measure the reading comprehension ability of an individual student or of a group. Test A is at approximately the nine-year-old or third-grade level; Test B is at approximately the 13-year-old or seventh-grade level. However, either test may be used with students of any age, including adults, to get some idea of reading comprehension ability.

The items originated with the National Assessment of Educational Progress, which administered each item all across the United States. Hence, you can compare your student with average third graders or average seventh graders.

The items cover a variety of reading comprehension skills. Although you cannot conclude that a student is weak in an area based on one item alone, the items indicate something about the student's abilities and give some suggestions for types of reading comprehension questions to use in drills.

Do not use the test items for teaching. You should not tell the student which items he or she got right or wrong, nor should you "go over" the test with the student. By doing so, you invalidate the use of the test for that student in the future. If you do not review the test with the student, you can use exactly the same test at a later time to show progress in reading ability.

You can make up your own comprehension questions similar to those in the test, using other materials. Since the question types discussed in the preceding pages will also guide you in writing your own comprehension questions, don't use the test items for teaching.

Idiomatic Expressions

Sometimes a student can't understand a phrase or a sentence because an idiomatic expression is used. An idiomatic expression is a group of words that has a meaning different from what those words usually mean. For example, "It is raining cats and dogs" doesn't mean that cats and dogs are coming down from the sky.

Some of these can be pictured humorously, and many have to be explained to students for whom English is a second language.

- **Time flies.**
- **She's over the hill.**
- **We don't see eye to eye.**
- **Go fly a kite.**
- **She has a green thumb.**
- **You put your foot in your mouth.**
- **Go jump in the lake.**
- **Keep a straight face.**
- **Throw your weight around.**
- **Eat your words.**
- **He really blew it.**
- **Pull the wool over her eyes.**
- **Keep the wolf from the door.**
- **He fell for her.**
- **She hit the roof.**
- **It brought down the house.**
- **Hit the books.**
- **She turned a cold shoulder to me.**
- **I look up to him.**
- **You see through him.**
- **That hit the nail on the head.**
- **Cut it out.**
- **Turn over a new leaf.**

Songs

Song lyrics are fun and useful to read. They help to teach reading because they often have much repetition. The student can memorize them and, hence, "read" them with ease and success. To make sure actual reading is taking place, take some words out of the song and write them on a piece of paper or a chalkboard or just point to random words in the song.

All librarians have songbooks if you want more songs for reading lessons. The following song came from a book called *Best Loved Songs of the American People* by Denes Agay.

She'll Be Comin' 'Round the Mountain

She'll be comin' 'round the mountain when she comes.
She'll be comin' 'round the mountain when she comes.
She'll be comin' 'round the mountain,
She'll be comin' 'round the mountain,
She'll be comin' 'round the mountain when she comes.

2. She'll be drivin' six white horses when she comes. (etc.)

3. Oh, we'll all go out to meet her when she comes. (etc.)

4. Oh, we'll kill the old red rooster when she comes. (etc.)

5. And we'll all have chicken and dumplins when she comes. (etc.)

Reading Ideas

- Get a library card!

- Check out a new book every week!

- Read a bit of the new book in the library before you take it home.

Step 4: Teach Vocabulary

Teaching vocabulary is usually divided into two quite different levels:

1. Beginning readers need to master a **basic sight vocabulary** of common words.
2. More advanced readers need **vocabulary improvement**, which means learning the meanings of new words.

Beginning readers, who for now we will define as any child or adult whose reading ability ranges from none to upper third grade, need to master a high-frequency vocabulary such as the Instant Words that are given at the end of this section. For example, they need to be able to read the first 300 Instant Words "instantly," without a moment's hesitation because these 300 words make up 65% of all written material. That's right; over half of every newspaper article, every textbook, every children's story, and every novel is composed of just these 300 words! These are words that occur over and over again—words like "the," "of," and "and." You can hardly write any sentence without using several of the first 300 Instant Words. And you certainly can't concentrate on comprehension if you are trying to figure out these basic words.

The table below shows that relatively few Instant Words make up a large percentage of all written material. Note that the column for 10 words is not any 10 words, but the first 10 Instant Words (likewise with the 100 and 300 words). Knowing the 1000 Instant Words allows you to read 90% of written material, but it takes a vocabulary of thousands of words to be a mature reader. This takes a lifetime of reading and learning. You have to start somewhere though, and these Instant Words give you an efficient start.

Percentage of written material composed of ranked Instant Words

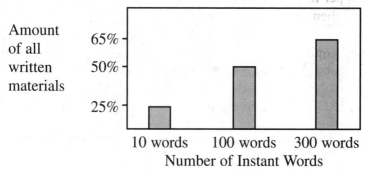

Another problem is that some of these often-used words do not follow regular phonics rules. For example, how do you sound out "of" or "said"? The answer is that beginning readers need to learn these words as "sight words."

The first part of this section will show you how to test your student to find out which of the Instant Words he or she knows, and then it will present some methods for teaching them. The second part of this section will discuss some vocabulary improvement techniques for students who have higher than a third-grade reading ability.

One of the important tools in every reading teacher's "bag of tricks" should be a list of the most frequently used words in reading. Children and adults who are just learning or who have failed to learn to read properly from regular instruction frequently have a very spotty reading vocabulary. They know some relatively uncommon words, but they do not know some of the words that appear most frequently. Take a moment to look over the list of Instant Words that you can use for teaching and testing on pages 108-113 in the Appendix.

Some basic reading textbooks have their own graded lists built into the series. If your student has not used a basic text series or else has learned only part of the list, you must "find out what the leaner knows."

Testing the Instant Words

To find out which Instant Words a student knows is easy. Use the Instant Words Test (pages 114 and 115) or simply ask him or her to read aloud from each column of the 600 Instant Words (pages 108-113). Then stop and teach the words he or she doesn't know.

If you have to work with groups, a way of diagnosing word knowledge for beginning readers is to make a recognition test. Copy a group of Instant Words, four words per line. Number the lines. Give each student a sheet with the words on it and then say, "On line 1 put an 'X' on the word 'you,' on line 2 put an 'X' on the word 'that,' " and so on. By correcting the tests, you can easily sort the pupils into groups for Instant Word instruction. Incidentally, save the tests and let students use them to study from or to review the words.

If you don't want to use this survey test, just have your student read every word on the Instant Word List, but not all at once—perhaps a column or part of a column at each lesson—until you have accumulated a set of unknown words that can be used for instruction.

Teaching the Instant Words

Since a high percentage of all reading material is composed of relatively few words, learning to read would appear to be a task which is ridiculously easy. If 300 words will do such a large percentage of the job, why not begin with just these words, teach them quickly, and get it over with at once? Unfortunately, it is not that easy.

Experience has shown that, normally, mastery of the first 300 Instant Words (or of any basic vocabulary list of this size, for that matter) could be expected to take nearly three years for primary children. An average student in an average school situation learns most of the first 100 words toward the end of the first year. The second hundred words are added during the second year. It is not until some time in the third year that all 300 words are really mastered and used as a part of the student's own reading vocabulary. This is not to deny that second and third graders can "read" many more words than the 300 Instant Words. They can also read many proper nouns and a smattering of subject words related to the type of material that they have been exposed to.

One California elementary school, which emphasized the teaching of the Instant Words as part of a well-balanced reading instruction program, was able to achieve the following results:

- At the end of kindergarten, 45% of the students could read 50 Instant Words.
- At the end of first grade, 76% of the students could read 150 Instant Words.
- At the end of second grade, 77% of the students could read 300 Instant Words.

One can expect to decrease the learning time required in the case of older students, illiterate adults, and students in upper elementary and secondary remedial reading classes. Still, their learning of the first 300 Instant Words is found to closely parallel their attained reading ability level. For example, a person who can just manage to read upper second-grade material knows most of the first 300 Instant Words.

A list of the 600 Instant Words is given in the Appendix. Make sure that your student knows most of the first 300 Instant Words "instantly" before proceeding to teach the second 300 Instant Words. The second 300 Instant Words are for reading and spelling lessons with students of fourth- and fifth-grade ability.

Methods for teaching the Instant Words vary with the teacher, the pupil, and the educational situation. Any method that works is a good method.

Use card games, easy reading practice, flash cards, and spelling lessons augmented by lavish praise, stern talks, competition, or a play-therapy climate. The pupil learns to read words in books, on flash cards, in his or her own compositions, or off wall charts. Teach him or her alone and in large groups, in the classroom. and out under the trees. All the while, three things are being conveyed by word and deed: (1) We care about the student. (2) We want the student to read. (3) These Instant Words are important.

Note that the Instant Words are in groups of five. This is to remind you that you shouldn't try to teach too many words at once. Some students can learn only two or three words per week, and others can "gobble down" 20. All need frequent review.

Easy Reading Practice

Easy reading practice is one of the best ways of teaching the Instant Words. For a student who can read on the second-grade level (whether with help or hesitatingly), "easy reading" is reading first-grade level materials. An excellent definition of easy reading material is printed matter in which a student can pronounce 99 percent of the words. Another rule of thumb is that when the student averages fewer than one mistake for every 20 words, the material is "easy" for him or her. Easy reading practice is especially beneficial because the material is certain to contain the Instant Words, and a student who barely knows these words gets practice in recognizing them. Easy reading practice helps a student to learn to apply context clues. Each reading gives the student a feeling of success, and encourages him or her to try to learn more.

Easy reading then is reading that is a grade or two below what the student "can" read. If a student can read at sixth-grade level, easy reading is at the fourth- or fifth-grade level. It is no accident that most popular novels are written at about the eighth-grade difficulty level while most book buyers are at least high school graduates.

Flash Cards

Many teachers, tutors, and parents use flash cards to help teach sight word reading. A flash card is simply a card with a word written on it. The word is written in bold print using a marker or dark crayon. Usually the print is in lowercase letters, like most of the words in this book.

A traditional way to teach using flash cards is to take a small number of words like five Instant Words. Tell the student each word and discuss it a little, perhaps using it in an oral sentence. Next, mix up the cards and "flash" them to the student while the student tries to quickly call out the word. If he or she misses, say the word (don't use phonics at this point). Mix up the words and flash them to the student again. After the student knows all the words, put them away, and at the next lesson, review them by flashing the cards and helping the student with any words he or she missed.

One of the nice things about flash cards is that they make great review lessons, and students often require much review of these words. Just because they have mastered the list one day, don't be surprised if they don't remember all the words next week. This is why review and more practice are needed. Incidentally, don't blame the student for forgetting. Instead, praise him or her for any words remembered and patiently teach the missed words. Everyone needs repetition when learning new words. Perhaps you need some repetitions in learning people's names or in learning new words connected with your business or in a new subject you are studying.

Another thing you can do with flash cards is to display them for referral at other times in the day. Teachers might line them up on the chalkboard, mothers might stick them on the refrigerator, and tutors might hand a small stack to the student to take home for practice.

Flash cards can also be used as sentence builders. Put two or three or more flash cards in order so that they make a phrase or a sentence. You can make some interesting sentences using rebuses. A "rebus" is simply a picture used instead of a word, for example:

The  **had a**  **.**

Read this as, "The girl had a dog."

Use flash cards with small groups. The teacher flashes the word as quickly as possible. The student who says the word first gets to hold the card. The point of the game is to see who gets the most cards. Another way to play the game is to give each student a turn at recognizing the word; when he or she misses, the next student gets a turn.

A student can also work alone with a small pack of flash cards, separating them into two piles: the cards known and those that are not known. When finished, the teacher or a more advanced student checks up on the "knows" pile and then helps the student with the "doesn't know" pile.

You can make your own flash cards on blank calling cards (obtained from a printer), on 3" x 5" cards, or on heavy card stock. You can copy the whole list, make cards for just the words the student misses when reading down the list, or purchase a set of Instant Words Flashcards. Remember, don't try to teach too many words at once. Keep the student's success rate high.

Bingo Game

Bingo is an excellent game for teaching Instant Words to large groups, but it is equally useful for small groups or even a single student. Twenty-five words can be placed on a card (five rows and five columns) in random order, with a card for each student. The words should be in a different order on each card. The teacher calls off the words in random order or draws the word cards out of a hat. Markers can be small squares of cardboard, bottle caps, beans, or anything handy. The first student to complete a row, column, or diagonal line wins.

Oftentimes, even though there has been a winner, the students like to play on until the board is filled and every word is covered. If the game is played until the board is filled, the teacher can sometimes spot poor readers by the number of uncovered words. In a teaching situation where some of the students do not know all the words, excellent instruction can ensue by having the teacher show the card or write the word on the board after saying it. This gives poor readers an equal chance at winning.

Note that by making five rows and five columns, one set of 25 Instant Words will fit on a card. For young children or beginning readers, you can make bingo cards with just nine words (three rows and three columns). Remember that each player must have a card with the same words, but arranged in a different order.

Sample Bingo Card

the	of	it	with	at
a	can	on	are	this
is	will	you	to	and
your	that	we	as	but
be	in	not	for	have

Pairs Game

Another game played with great success is called Pairs. Pairs is played like Rummy or Fish, except that only two cards are needed to make a book or pair. Two to five persons may play. Five cards are dealt to each player, and the remainder of the deck is placed in the center of the table. The object of the game is to get as many pairs as possible. There are only two cards alike in each deck.

The player to the right of the dealer may ask any one other player for a specific card. For example, "Do you have 'and'?" The player asking must have the mate (in the example, the "and" card) in his or her hand. The player who is asked must give up the card if he or she has it. If the first player does not get the card asked for, he or she draws one card from the pile. Then the next player has a turn at asking for a card.

If the player succeeds in getting the card asked for, either from another player or from the pile, he or she gets another turn. If the player gets a pair, it is placed down in front of him or her. The player with the most pairs at the end of the game wins. If the player **doing the asking** does not know how to read the word on the card, he or she may show the card and ask any of the other players or anyone present.

If the player **who is asked** for a card does not know how to read that word or is unsure of himself, the best thing to do is ask to see the card of the player requesting the card or ask a non-playing person who can read to look at his or her hand.

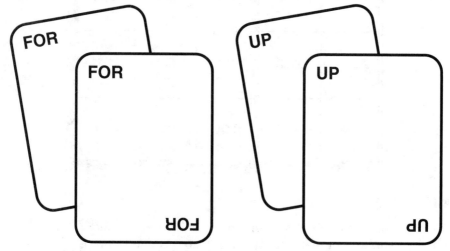

Make two cards for each word in a Pairs game deck.

The students should know some but not all the words used in a particular deck. They should have help in playing until they know almost all the words and can get along by themselves. They can usually accomplish this quite rapidly as the game is highly motivating. The students should play the game on several different occasions until they can call out all the words instantly. They should then move to the next harder deck. Reviewing easier decks is also recommended.

Make the card decks with groups of 25 Instant Words; two cards for each word makes a 50-card deck. Your student can help you make the decks. Make the decks for the level of words your student needs to learn.

Once in a while, it is good to review easy words already mastered, just for fun. But, generally, instructional games should follow the same rules as those set up for the selection of instructional reading material, i.e., not too easy and not too hard.

Concentration Game

The Pairs decks can also be used to play a Concentration game. Take a deck of 50 cards and place them facedown spread out over a table in mixed-up order. One to four persons can play. Each player turns over two cards. If they are a pair, he or she keeps them. If they are not a pair, then they must be put back in exactly the same place, facedown. The trick of the game is to remember the location of cards so one can make a pair with each two cards turned up. From a reading instruction standpoint, the students must read aloud each card turned over. If he or she doesn't know how to read the card, another player can read the word aloud.

Spelling

The Instant Words may be used for spelling lessons, particularly words which the students have trouble learning to read. For student writing the Instant Words are just as important as they are for reading. You can't write any story without using some of the Instant Words. A typical spelling lesson has these elements:

1. The student is shown the words to be learned on a chalkboard, on flash cards, or on a piece of paper. He or she is asked to read them aloud and sometimes use them in sentences orally so you are sure that the student knows how to pronounce them and knows their meanings.

2. The student may copy the words or write them in a sentence.

3. The student is given a trial test, which means the teacher says the word and the student tries to write it.

4. The student's trial test is corrected, and each incorrect letter or missing letter is circled or added.

5. The student studies the errors and practices writing the words correctly.

6. The final spelling test is given. Any words containing mistakes are added to next week's spelling list.

Don't give too many words in a spelling lesson. For example, five to 10 words for a beginner (first-grade level) and 20 words for grade levels three to six is enough.

Here is a suggested spelling study method for students:

Word Study Method for Students

1. <u>Look</u> at the whole word carefully.

2. <u>Say</u> the word aloud to yourself.

3. <u>Spell</u> say each letter to yourself.

4. <u>Write</u> the word from memory. (Cover the word and write it.)

5. <u>Check</u> your written word against the correct spelling.
   (Circle errors and repeat Steps 4 and 5.)

For more information on teaching spelling and 195 weekly spelling lessons covering difficulty levels grades one to six, see the *Spelling Book* published by Teacher Created Materials.

Picture Nouns

Picture Nouns are a 100-word list at the end of this section intended to supplement the Instant Words. They are words that can easily be pictured and are words that students need when writing stories. The Instant Words do not have too many "subject words," those words that tell about the content.

The Picture Nouns can be taught along with the Instant Words, a group of five at a time. They are particularly useful in using flash cards as sentence builders, and the picture side of the card can be used as a rebus (picture for a word in a sentence).

Picture Nouns can also be used in "thinking skills." Take two or more groups of five Picture Nouns, mix them up, and have the student sort them into piles that belong together. It makes the student "think," and gives him or her practice reading words.

The Picture Nouns can also be used in self-teaching lessons. Give the student a stack of cards with the word sides up. The student tries to read the word, and if he or she can't, the card is turned over in order to look at the picture.

Most of the games and techniques used in teaching the Instant Words can also be used with the Picture Nouns. For ready-to-use Picture Noun cards, see the book *Picture Nouns* (TCM 2763) or *Picture Nouns Flash Cards* (TCM 2765).

 car

 boat

Vocabulary Building

"Vocabulary building" is used mostly for more advanced students, such as those students of any age who are reading better than third-grade difficulty level. Basically, these are students who recognize instantly most of the first 300 Instant Words and who have a fair grasp of basic phonics skills.

Pay Attention

The first rule in vocabulary building is **when you encounter a new word while reading, pause and pay attention to it.** See if you can get the meaning of the word from the way it is used in the sentence. If you can't, ask someone or "ask" the dictionary.

Direct Instruction

A second major method of new vocabulary learning is direct instruction for new words. Some teachers and families put up a new word a day on the chalkboard, a bulletin board, or a card on the table, and discuss it briefly. For example, you might put up "inclement" on a rainy day, or "torrid" on a hot day. Maybe the new word comes from hearing it used on TV or in a newspaper, like "seismograph" when describing earthquakes or "coup" when reporting revolutions.

Prefixes and Roots

Learning to use word prefixes and roots is also a good way to expand vocabulary. Even little children know that "un" in front of a word changes its meaning, as in "unhappy," and they can extend this to learning the meaning of "unable." The same idea applies to word roots. For example, "tele" means "far," so "television" means seeing something that is far away. This root is also seen in "telescope," "telegram," etc. and helps to explain the meanings of those words.

A list of some common prefixes and roots can be found in the Appendix on pages 118-122. In addition, most large dictionaries give the root meanings of words, which can help you learn the meaning of that word and other words that use that root.

Use New Words

Finally, you should keep in mind that learning new words is a lifelong task. Every time you start to learn a new subject or read a new book, you will encounter new words to be learned. Welcome the task and enjoy it. It will also help to learn new words if you try to use them in speech and writing.

Encourage your student to try using any new word. Praise him or her for using a new word, even if it is mispronounced or misspelled. After all, it is through using words that they become a permanent part of one's vocabulary.

Vocabulary Building

1. Pay attention to new words.

2. Ask someone their meanings.

3. Look them up in a dictionary.

4. Learn a new word a day.

5. Study prefixes and roots.

6. Use new words often.

Homophones

These are words which sound alike but have a different spelling and a different meaning. They use to be called "homonyms." They cause some trouble for beginning readers and beginning writers (spellers). Some common errors are:

to—two—too

there—their—they're

right—write

wood—would

for—four

For a list of more homophones, see page 123 in the Appendix. You can teach homophones as part of a reading or writing lesson by calling attention to them as they occur, or you can have short homophone lessons using spelling lessons, flash cards (one homophone on each side), or games.

Step 5: Develop Phonics Skills

You are doing a lot for your student. You have found his or her reading level and have provided materials in which he or she can succeed in reading. You are encouraging the student to practice reading, checking comprehension, and helping him or her develop a basic reading vocabulary with the Instant Words.

You can help in still another way. You can help your student improve his or her reading by building phonics skills. The following pages will prepare you to use the Phonics Survey and the Phonics Charts effectively.

Place of Teaching Phonics

Teachers, like parents, often take positions "for" and "against" phonics. Interestingly enough, neither side can conclusively prove the "phonics method" is better or worse than the "word method." Hence, most teachers teach both. I suggest that you do the same.

On the charts in the Appendix, beginning on page 125, you will find most of the basic phonics rules arranged in a good order for teaching. Some teachers who emphasize phonics start on the first day of school and drill students on letter sounds and example words. They make sure to get through all these rules in the first grade.

A phonics moderate would start phonics lessons after the student had acquired a small sight-word vocabulary (25 or 50 words). He or she would probably try to teach the material in the first few charts during the first year but would not be too upset with less than perfect performance.

A phonics laggard would take three years to cover the material in these charts and probably would skip over much of the material in Charts 6 and 7 on pages 130 and 131. Some basic reading series are in this category.

These "years" refer to children beginning at age six with average ability. Bright children, older children, and adults would, of course, go faster. And all can benefit from some review on phonics as part of reading or spelling lessons

Learning the Alphabet

Most children learn to read and write the alphabet in kindergarten or first grade. Some learn it in preschool or at home. Illiterate adults need to learn the alphabet early in their instruction cycle.

Learning the alphabet is often considered a pre-reading skill. But it is not absolutely necessary to know the alphabet before simple reading instruction begins. In other words, it is quite possible to read whole little books without knowing the names of all the letters. However, it is quite necessary to know the alphabet before beginning phonics instruction.

You can teach the alphabet a lot of different ways. Little children use alphabet picture books. Teachers select several different letters and ask the students to say them. You can teach the "alphabet song." You can put the letters on flash cards (capitals on one side and lowercase letters on the other side) and have flashing drills or put them in pocket charts. Test your students' alphabet knowledge by pointing to letters and asking them to say the letter names.

Writing the Alphabet

Teaching students to read the alphabet (learning letter names) is often accompanied by learning to write the alphabet. Children are usually taught the capital manuscript (printing) letters first, followed by the lowercase letters.

Cursive handwriting (connected letters) is usually taught in the third grade. It is not necessary to teach cursive writing as almost all writing tasks can be done using manuscript. In fact, manuscript handwritring is often required on various forms such as job applications or post office forms. It is even legal to use manuscript for signatures on checks. Manuscript writing is just as fast as cursive and often more legible. However, there is some advantage in knowing how to read other people's cursive handwriting. When schools have tried to teach manuscript handwriting only, it is often the pressure from parents or simple tradition which makes them teach cursive, not educational necessity.

To teach writing the alphabet, select several letters and demonstrate how they are written using the chalkboard or a piece of paper. It helps beginning students to have lined paper. The handwriting charts in the Appendix on page 141 show stroking lines (how you start to write the letter).

Ask the student to copy the letters. It usually takes a bit of practice on each letter. When the students have some familiarity with writing the letters, you can have a "letter" spelling test. Call out letter names and see if the students can write them. The students will enjoy writing simple words or their names using letters they have just learned.

Phoneme Awareness

All teachers would agree on the importance of first being sure that the student can make the speech sounds and can hear the differences between sounds. Children need to develop a skill called "phoneme awareness." This means knowing that all words are made up of relatively few sounds. The English language uses about 44 phoneme sounds. For example, "cat" has three phonemes, /k/, /ă/, /t/. "Phonics" is learning the correlation between the spoken sound and its spelling or, in other words, the sound at the beginning of the word "cat" is spelled with a "c," the /ă/ sound with an "a," etc.

You can help develop this phoneme awareness by reading to your student poems and stories that have repetitions of sounds (like *Cat in the Hat*), by pointing out the same sound in similar words (see the Phonics Charts on pages 125-133 in the Appendix), and by other word patterns such as phonograms (see the list of phonograms on pages 134-137 in the Appendix).

Note that in teaching "phoneme awareness" we are not teaching reading or "phonics." We are simply helping the student get ready for phonics. To do this, the student needs to become aware that sounds (phonemes) change. Here are a few examples.

Initial Consonant Change

cat

tat

rat

hat

sat

Final Consonant Change

mad

mat

mack

man

mass

Vowel Change

mad – mud

hat – hit

bit – bet

top – tip

rash – rush

Since in phoneme awareness you are not teaching reading, most phoneme awareness can be done orally, using no printed words. Simply say the words and see if the students can hear the difference. Make the phonene in isolation. For example, say, "top /t/, /o/, /p/" and "tip /t/, /i/, /p/." Let the student say the word then each phoneme.

Using the phoneme awareness charts for guidance, work your way up to more complicated words like:

from /f/, /r/, /u/, /m/	**these** /th/, /ē/, /z/
out /ou/, /t/	**duty** /d/, /o͞o/, /t/, /ē/
stop /s/, /t/, /o/, /p/	**jump** /j/, /u/, /m/, /p/

Of course, the student will develop more phoneme awareness as reading, spelling, and phonics skills develop. But you can teach some phoneme awareness before reading instruction begins.

Phonics Instruction

Phonics means knowing the correspondence between printed letters (graphemes) and their sounds (phonemes). As previously mentioned in the Phoneme Awareness section, words are composed of different sounds (phonemes). There are only about 44 phonemes in the English language, but there are several ways to spell some of them. For example, the long /a/ sound can be spelled "ay" as in "say" or "ai" as in "aid" or even "a" with the silent "e" at the end of a word as in "made." In contrast, the /b/ sound heard at the beginning of "boy" is nearly always spelled with the letter "b."

Unfortunately, we have only a 26-letter alphabet so there is not one letter for each phoneme. All the vowels have two or more sounds, but the consonants are more polite since many of them tend to have one main way of spelling (i.e., a single letter represents the phoneme).

However, the teaching of phonics is not hopelessly complicated. The Phonics Charts in the Appendix contain nearly all of the phonics most readers need to know, and many people can read or spell quite well without knowing many of these phonics rules.

Whether or not to say the sounds in isolation is a problem you can solve for yourself. Personally, I do, but I am careful not to use a "schwa" sound ("uh") at the end of a consonant when it isn't needed. For example, I say, "nnn," not "nuh." Consonants that can be pronounced without a schwa are "T," "N," "R," "M," "S," "L," "P," "F," "V," "H," "K," "W," and the digraphs (two letters making one sound).

Some teachers say the sounds should only be taught as part of a word. Others say it is all right to pronounce a consonant with a vowel, but this group is divided (c-at or ca-t). The important point of phonics is that the student must learn that the letter or digraph stands for a sound. It is also helpful to learn common letter clusters like "-ump", to read and spell words like "bump," "clump," "dump," etc. These word families are called phonograms. You will see a good variety of phonograms on pages 134-137 in the Appendix.

Diagnosing Phonics Skills

In phonics, as in everything else, a good teacher must know where a student is at the beginning, middle, and end of instruction.

For a simple test you can write a letter or digraph (like "sh") on the board and ask the student what sound it makes. Or you can ask him or her to sound out some nonsense syllable, building into the nonsense word the thing you want to test. For example, if you want to know if the student knows the digraphs on Chart 4 (page 128), write "phiz," and if he or she says "fizz," you know that he or she knows some phonics.

The Phonics Survey on pages 138 and 139 will help you systematically test skills in the main phonics areas.

Methods of Teaching Phonics

Phonics Charts

The Phonics Charts on pages 125-133 give you a rather complete overview of what is usually taught in phonics in most schools. The Phonics Charts are arranged in a teaching order, so it is suggested that you teach the content of the first chart, then the second chart, etc.

In phonics you are just trying to teach the letter-sound connection. Don't worry if your student can't read all the words on the charts. The words and pictures are there just so that there will be some examples of the sounds that the letter makes in a word.

Sometimes it takes two letters to make one sound. These two-letter combinations are called "digraphs" and should be taught just as if the digraph was a single letter. For example, the digraph "sh" consists of "s" and "h" but produces a different sound (phoneme). "Blends" like the "bl" at the beginning of "black" are given in the last chart. Blends have two or three phonemes.

You will also note that some consonants (e.g., "c" and "g") and all vowels have several sounds. This is confusing for the student and requires a little practice. If he or she slowly masters the skills as they are presented in the order of these charts, it will cut down on the confusion.

Encourage your student to apply phonics when he or she is reading and can't pronounce a word. You can say, "Try sounding it out." Help him or her to do this. However, when trying to sound out unknown words, you will quickly find that phonics rules don't always work. There are more rules than are presented on these charts, and beyond that there are many exceptions. Why should "sugar" have an "sh" sound at the beginning, or why does "of" have an /uv/ sound? There just aren't enough rules to cover these things, and that is why *many words have to be learned as sight words.* But do not despair; phonics does help in unlocking many words and phonics rules are also useful in some spelling lessons. Phonics rules often help the student to sound out just part of the word, too. With this much information, plus context (how the word is used in a sentence), the student can often get the word. For example, the first thing many reading teachers say when a student is stuck on a word is, "What sound does it begin with?"

Nobody ever said that it was easy to learn how to read. It takes time and practice spread out over years. Your student needs all the help he or she can get, and phonics is just one way to help a little. You can use the Phonics Charts to introduce some phonics skills like Easy Consonants or Short Vowels, then give a lot of practice using them with practice words, games, and calling attention to these elements when reading.

Bingo

I have always liked to teach phonics with games. A game that works well for phonics is Bingo. Make some Bingo cards of the sound on Chart 1 (page 125) and call off the letters sounds, one at a time. (Don't use letter names—say "k as in cat" not "cee.") You can also make different "pairs" games, teaching the children to use consonant sounds instead of Instant Words.

Bingo Card for Beginners

T	N	R
M	D	S
L	C	P

Bingo Card for More Advanced Students

B	F	V	A	H
K	W	J	QU	X
Y	Z	TH	CH	WH
SH	PH	PR	ST	PL
TW	GL	SN	FR	SK

Remember when making Bingo cards that every player must have the same letters but in different arrangements. When calling letters, remember to use letter sounds. Say, "/s/ as in Sam," not the letter name such as "dee (d)," "es (s)" "are (r)," etc.

Spelling

Some teachers are quite successful teaching phonics along with spelling and writing. After an initial presentation of the first half of Phonics Charts 1 and 2, such a teacher might say, "Class, write *sad* on your papers." (Note that this gives every student a chance to participate.) After a minute, she has a pupil write the word correctly on the board. Then each student gets immediate knowledge of results to help his or her learning. Of course, the teacher chooses just phonetically regular words from among the sounds already introduced.

Some teachers might even call off nonsense words, such as "dat" and "nuv," just to test the pupils' abilities in phonics. Other teachers are more concerned that students know the meaning of each word, and whenever possible, have students use each word in a sentence.

The *Spelling Book* mentioned earlier contains a lot of phonics instruction suggestions, which shows that phonics can easily and effectively be taught in spelling lessons. As a teacher or tutor, you can take your choice and teach phonics as part of reading lessons, as part of spelling lessons, or both, which might be even better.

Phonograms

A phonogram is a group of letters containing a vowel and a consonant sound that needs another consonant sound to make a word. For example, the "-ail" phonogram can make words like "mail," "tail," and "sail" when different consonants are added.

Phonograms or word families, as they are sometimes called, make interesting and fun lessons for phonemic awareness (sound only), reading lessons (reading, printed words), and spelling lessons. Here are some phonogram families.

–ay	–ill	–at	–y
bay	bill	bat	by
day	fill	cat	my
hay	hill	fat	cry
pay	pill	mat	dry

In the Appendix on pages 134-137, you will find a list of phonograms and example words that you can use in teaching. There are many more phonograms, but these will get you started.

One way to teach a phonogram is simply to write it on a piece of paper or chalkboard, then ask your student how many words he or she can make using that phonogram. You can help a little, as needed.

Phonogram lists also make interesting spelling lessons. Give one or two phonogram families to your student, help him or her study them a little, making sure that he or she can pronounce all the words, then give a spelling test to see if he or she can spell them all. This is a great way to teach the sounds of different consonants and, hence, phonograms.

Phonograms also can be taught with many games and teaching devices. Word wheels, slide charts, and board games often use phonograms. These devices can be teacher made, student made, or bought in school supply stores.

"Phonogram" is a reading teacher word. Some researchers call the same idea "onset and rime." The "onset" is the initial consonant sound like "d-" and the "rime" is the ending vowel and consonant like "-og." Together they make "dog," which rhymes with "log," "fog," "bog," etc. Some linguists call the same idea "consonant substitution." Whatever you call it, try some of the examples on pages 134-137 for reading and spelling lessons.

You might want to start your phonics lessons by using the Phonics Survey on pages 138 and 139. You can get a good idea of a student's phonics ability by asking him or her to "sound out" unknown words. If sounding out a whole word is too difficult, you can just say "What sound does it begin with?" Or, "Do you know some other words that have parts that sound like parts of this word?" Phonics Charts 1–9 (pages 125-133) suggest a good teaching order that is based on frequency.

Phonics Warning

The good part of phonics is that it helps the student to sound out unknown words and make rapid progress in reading. The bad part of phonics is that some teachers "beat it to death" with boring drills, and the student learns to hate reading and education in general.

Another caution about phonics is that if too much emphasis is placed on sounds and not enough on other skills in reading, such as comprehension, then children can become word-callers. They spit out the words orally but have no idea what they mean. So balance your lessons. Do some word drill, some oral reading, some phonics, some silent reading, some comprehension drills, some spelling and writing lessons, and lots of easy reading in interesting books.

Step 6: Writing, Speaking, Listening

Some years ago in Africa I saw what I shall always think of as the minimum school. It consisted of a tree, a chair, and a small box of books. There was no furniture for the students; they sat on the bare ground. This school had no walls, no windows, no electricity, no chalkboard, no basal readers, practically no library, and no pencils or paper. I often think of it when I hear teachers complain about a lack of books or supplies.

Yet this minimum school had many advantages. The setting was beautiful: birds sang, and butterflies floated through the classroom. The air was fresh and the lighting excellent. No bells rang to end lessons, and no principal provided rules. The teacher had to be creative, and he was. He was conducting a very good elementary reading lesson. "How?" you might ask, when he had nothing. Well, he didn't quite have nothing. Most importantly, he had some knowledge of teaching techniques, and secondly, he had a long, straight stick.

He had the students take the stick and smooth a section of bare ground. Then, with a twig plucked from a nearby bush, he had the students draw lines in the dirt, using the stick as a ruler. And on those lines students wrote stories in small groups: one student writing, others helping with spelling and story suggestions, then all students reading the story when it was written. The students were divided into groups, and one group read the other groups' stories and talked about them.

The teacher helped the students get started, aided in correcting spelling and grammar, and, of course, provided the atmosphere for creative writing and the discipline that got the story written and read. He also later had most of the students write some of the words used in the story with their own twigs in the smoothed dirt.

The children were very proud to show me their stories, and I have been grateful for the rest of my life for the experience. Never again will I take too seriously a teacher's complaints that he or she can't teach reading well because there aren't enough books or supplies, or the chalkboard or classroom isn't in good shape.

Language Experience Approach

The teaching method the African teacher used is well known is the United States and is called various names, such as the "language experience approach" or part of the "whole language method" because it integrates reading, writing, speaking, and listening. Teachers in the United States usually have chalkboards, paper charts with felt tip pens, pencils, and paper, or computers with word processing programs, but the basic ideas are the same as the African teacher with his twigs and dirt.

1. Motivate the student (or a group) to write a story.

2. Have most students read the story.

3. Discuss it, extend it, and correct it.

Sounds simple, doesn't it? Why, then, doesn't everybody use it all the time? There are a lot of reasons. Some teachers find it hard to get students to be creative writers all the time. Using books extends the students' reading and thinking experiences. Some students do better with a more structured approach, which might include basic sight vocabularies, phonics, and varieties of comprehension questions. But a lot of teachers use storywriting for part of their reading lessons. And you can, too.

Story Starters

To get a story out of a student or a group, the teacher often has to help the writing get started. Some teachers use a recent, common experience like rain on the playground, a trip to the zoo, a job change.

Another technique for getting stories started is to use a story starter, which is a phrase or a suggested title:

> My favorite place to be. . .
> Don't you hate it when. . .
> In the year 2020. . .

There are more story starters in the Appendix (page 140), and you can probably think up some of your own. Also, as suggested earlier, some of the items in the Interest Inventories in the Appendix (pages 92 and 93) can be used as story starters.

Experience Charts

One method of storywriting that is used more with beginning readers who do not have much writing ability is for the teacher to do the writing on a large piece of paper or a chalkboard as the students dictate a story. This can be done with a single student or a small group. It can be done with very beginning readers, children or adults with no reading ability, or with students with some reading ability.

The basic idea is that the students tell a short story while the teacher or tutor writes it down. Then the students read the story to the teacher. To get started, the student can suggest a title, or the teacher can provide a bit of motivation by using a story starter. After a title is written down, the teacher can help the dictation by saying something like, "Now, what do you want to say about. . .?"

The teacher must be careful to write in short, easy sentences. It is all right for the teacher to modify the student's dictation a bit by writing correct grammar and using easy vocabulary. Especially in the beginning, the story should be short. Remember, the student or students are going to have to read back the whole story and learn to read all the new words used.

The story need not be completed in one lesson. The teacher might just write a sentence or two, then add to the story the next day. Of course, each day the previous parts of the story are reviewed with the student trying to read it, with help from the teacher only as necessary.

The teacher should take words out of the story and see if the student can read them. This prevents students from just memorizing the whole story and not really knowing how to read the individual words. It is not bad for the student to become so familiar with a story that it is almost memorized, but it is a good reading lesson to make sure that the student also knows how to read each of the words in the story. Take a look again at the Step 4 chapter for other techniques for teaching individual words.

You should also do some kind of comprehension check on the story just so the student gets the idea that for all reading, comprehension is essential. The Step 3 chapter has suggestions on varying the types of questions and other comprehension teaching techniques.

Writing the students' stories on a sheet of paper or on a large paper chart has one advantage over a chalkboard: they can be saved and read later, at the end of a week, or a month, or even a year. Sometimes students like to look back at their earlier lessons to see how far they have come in reading more advanced material.

But with Experience Charts, as with any other type of lesson, keep it easy enough to be successful. Frustrate your student too often, and you won't have a student; you might have a body, but the mind will be elsewhere.

Student-written Stories

As students develop more skills in writing, they can write their own stories, using paper and pencil. Schools often use lined paper with wider lines for young children, but this is not necessary. Most schools now urge student writers to use "invented spelling" on their first draft. This means that the student should write the story to get the ideas down and worry about correct spelling later. This same is true for grammar. It can be corrected on a later draft.

Not every story has to be polished. Sometimes the student can just write a short, interesting story and read it to the teacher or to the class. Other times the student should polish a story more by having the teacher or an advanced student look it over and suggest better spelling or better grammar.

Incidentally, writing is developmental, just like reading and speaking. In speaking, for example, the child first babbles, then has one-word sentences, and then simple vocabulary and slightly longer sentences. At first, speech sounds are not complete, and some words come out mispronounced in "baby talk." The same things happen in writing, but at an older age. Writing development goes from scribbling, to crude letters, to invented spelling, to short stories with simple vocabulary, and later to more mature writing. Help children progress a little bit at a time. Give them a lot of encouragement at any stage, and don't overly criticize mistakes. Not every story needs to be a showpiece. Get the ideas down. Practice makes for writing fluency.

Older students and adults might enjoy writing whole little books composed of a collection of stories. Some teachers type these student stories and bind them along with student art for illustrations. If you have several students, they can read each other's stories or books.

Handwriting

On page 141 in the Appendix are Handwriting Charts that can be used to teach handwriting. For beginners, it is not too hard. Just have them practice on a few letters at a time, using the manuscript alphabet. Then they can combine the letters into words. All beginners need occasional correction and sometimes more practice on certain letters that they form poorly when writing stories.

For most children, handwriting instruction begins at home or in kindergarten using capital (block) letters. Next they progress to lowercase letters and then to slanted manuscript letters.

There are several popular systems of forming letters. The stroking arrows on the handwriting charts in the Appendix are one popular way of teaching beginning handwriting, but most other systems work well also. Most schools will give anyone a copy of the handwriting chart they are using.

In most public schools, somewhere near the end of second grade or the beginning of third grade, the students are taught the cursive alphabet, which most adults use for everyday writing.

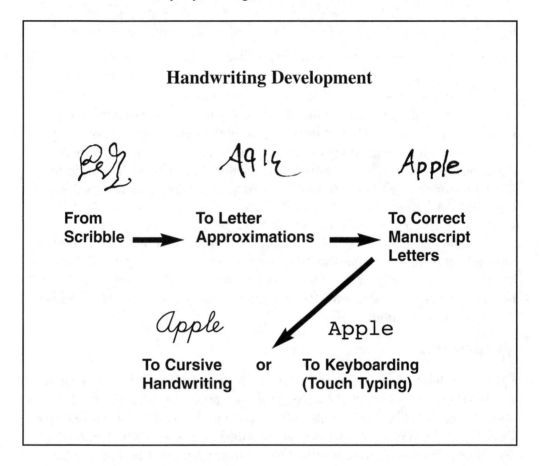

When students reach third- or fourth-grade ability, they may be taught to type using the regular 10-finger ("touch") system. This is not hard to do. It only takes about four weeks of lessons. If you want to try it, get a typewriter or a computer with a word-processing program and follow the lesson in *Computer Keyboarding for Beginners* (TCM 2764). Because the lessons in this book are based on the Instant Words lists, learning to keyboard with this method reinforces sight vocabulary and spelling instruction. It works for adults, too. High-school remedial students often feel that learning to type makes their reading and writing lessons more "adult."

An argument in favor of teaching typing, or "keyboarding," is that in the near future many jobs will require keyboarding skills. Also, in some high schools and colleges, papers must be typed and often computers are used for homework. We have taught many children between fourth grade and junior high age and found that it just takes a little discipline and practice to learn a skill that will be of great value for a lifetime.

Expository Writing

We have been talking about writing as though "stories" are the only things students write or read. This is not so. Expository writing means non-story writing. It includes such things as autobiographies, news stories, textbooks, directions, filling out forms, and advertisements. Your student will need to know how to do this type of writing also, as well as having some practice with this type of reading.

Adult literacy students especially appreciate the functional need for expository writing and reading. In many adult classes, the writing is very practical. Students fill out job applications, post office forms, and work reports. Learning to write helps learning to read, and learning to read helps learning to write. So, practice both.

Speaking

Speaking is oral composition of words just as writing is written composition of words. It will help your student's writing if he or she is given plenty of opportunities to talk. Sometimes, just let your student tell a story or describe something. Encourage the development of ideas and use of new words. Do not make fun or joke about incorrect words use; sometimes permit it, and sometimes gently suggest a more correct word use. It is through experimenting and trying out that we all learned to talk and, hopefully, are still learning to talk because, like reading and writing, speaking is a lifelong developmental process. So, encourage use of new or partially known words. Encourage wild ideas and conventional ideas. Take some time to just listen to your student.

Incidentally, don't get too excited about speech errors or "baby talk," especially with young children or ESL students. It is normal for children to not be able to make all the English speech sounds (phonemes) until about age six. It is also normal for children coming from homes where another language is spoken to not be able to make all the English speech sounds. For example, the Spanish language has no /j/ sound that we hear at the beginning of "general." Note that the Spanish boy's name "Juan" sounds like it begins with a "w" sound. Every language in the world has a slightly different set of speech sounds (phonemes), so don't expect perfect enunciation for young children or ESL students, but you can gently suggest correction. Since all speech sounds are based on mechanical mouth positions and breath, you can often help correct speech errors by simply letting the student see you form the letters and then look in a mirror to see himself or herself making the sound. The Phonics Charts can give you some practice words for most speech sounds.

If your student hasn't shown definite progress after a year, you might consult the speech therapist in your local public school (even if your student goes to a private school). But the first rule is "don't get excited" on discovering any speech problem and don't rush off to all sorts of specialists and make a big deal out of it. Most students grow out of speech problems, especially if you help them a little. In the meantime, do not, under any circumstances, embarrass them.

Listening

We all learn to talk by listening. If our mothers, fathers, and playmates all spoke Chinese, we would all speak Chinese. But beyond this basic fact, listening to stories read to us helps us to talk better, read better, and write better. So many educators recommend that you **read to students every day**.

Many parents read daily to their preschoolers and that is an excellent idea, but unfortunately they stop when the child gets into elementary school. When I was a sixth-grade teacher, I read several whole books to my class, a little bit each day, and they loved it. You are never too old to listen. There are several very successful companies selling "books on tape." They sell these not to the blind or illiterate or to young children but to business executives to listen to in their cars while commuting or in their bathrooms while shaving. In many public libraries you can check out audio tapes of both children's stories and adult books. But for children, there is nothing like having a parent or a teacher read to them.

While books and stories are usually used for listening experiences, you can also read all sorts of material, like news articles or directions.

Listening is good for students for the following reasons:

1. It improves vocabulary. They learn word use, and they hear words that might not be in everyday speech.

2. It improves grammar because they hear correct usage and variety in sentence construction.

3. It expands their thinking. They are temporarily transported to the world of tigers, spaceships, or different kinds of families. They see that language can be fun.

4. Students can listen to harder stories than they can read for themselves, so there is an expanded choice of reading material. (One long-term goal of reading instruction is that they be able to read for themselves anything that they can understand by listening.)

So, if you don't do anything else suggested in this book—if you don't give any tests, don't teach any phonics or Instant Words, don't ask any comprehension questions, or don't require any written stories—the least you can do is read to your student(s).

Listening Comprehension

You can check listening comprehension by asking the student to retell all or part of the story, responding orally or in writing. Comprehension lessons can also be done by the teacher reading a passage from a comprehension drill book page and having the student answer the questions. The *Nonfiction Comprehension Test Practice* books published by Teacher Created Materials (TCM 3509-3513) have sample passages for students with reading abilities ranging from grades 2 through 6.

Conclusion

The six steps presented in this book should give you enough information to help you start teaching reading. They also give some additional suggestions for improvement if you already have some experience teaching reading. Actually, the six steps are the basic techniques used by many experienced classroom and remedial reading teachers for both children and adults.

Ideas for Teaching Reading

I recently had the pleasant experience of editing a book entitled *The 10 Best Ideas for Reading Teachers*, in which 44 nationally recognized reading experts gave some of their best ideas about teaching reading. Practically every idea mentioned in the preceding sections was mentioned by at least several of those reading specialists. Here are a few additional ideas of theirs that you can use:

- Use reading materials from other school subjects like science or social studies.

- Include drama (plays) for oral reading, speaking, and listening experiences.

- Have students write every day. For example, have them keep a journal or diary, write summaries of what they've read, or write a letter to a friend.

- Parents and teachers should set a good example by reading themselves, often. Some suggest a regular quiet time for reading.

- Use graphic organizers, like making a time line for history or directions, a flow chart of a story, or a cluster of characteristics associated with a vocabulary word.

- Let students use a computer with a word processor or a typewriter for storywriting. (If you do, please teach your student to type with the 10-finger method.)

- Encourage students to join a book club.

- Try using captioned television to teach reading.

- Have students read the same story over and over again, not just until oral errors disappear but until reasonable speed and fluency appear.

- Occasionally repeat assessment tasks like the Oral Reading, Phonics Survey, or the Silent Reading Tests.

- If you spot reading problems, tackle them early; don't wait.

- Allow students to read for pleasure, read about real things, and read logos (like Coca Cola®, Kleenex®, etc.).

- Expand students' vocabulary any way you can: by reading, speaking, and picking words out of reading selections and discussing them.

- Emphasize comprehension. Form questions before, during, and after reading. Ask the students to recall, summarize, and compare.

- Develop background knowledge about a reading selection; talk about the setting, the characters, similar circumstances, or similar subject matter.

- Remember that students are all different. They develop at different rates, have different interests, and have different abilities.

- Get a joke book. Read one a day.

- Don't forget that learning to read is a complex, lifelong process. You are not going to develop a mature reader in one month or even one year, but you can certainly move your student ahead a notch in that length of time and that, after all, is all any teacher can do.

The Last Word

For teacher and students alike, there is no substitute for practice. Hence, you should practice teaching reading and practice improving your technique. After you practice teaching reading, reread applicable portions of this book. You may find them even more helpful after you are face to face teaching a real live student.

Last, but not least, I'd like to say that the ability to teach reading is a wonderful skill. When you teach a child or an illiterate adult how to read, you have given him or her a priceless gift that will keep on giving for a lifetime.

Appendix

Oral Reading Test: Directions

The student reads aloud from one copy of the test while the examiner marks another copy. The student copy of the Oral Reading Test is on pages 85-87.

The examiner can make a copy of the Oral Reading Test: Examiner's Copy and Record Sheet (pages 88-91) or just use the copy in this book for scoring. The examiner asks the student to begin reading from the student's copy while he or she follows along using the examiner's copy.

Scoring

Count one mistake for each word the student is unable to pronounce. If he or she immediately corrects the error, this is not counted as a mistake. If a student omits a word, ask him or her to read the line again more carefully.

Underline each word the student can't pronounce or needs help in pronouncing. When the student has finished reading a paragraph, count the mistakes and check the appropriate line to the right of each paragraph.

For example, if a student begins with Paragraph 1-B and reads it without a mistake or with one or two mistakes, he or she can read at this level independently. Check "Independent" to the right of the paragraph.

The student should then read Paragraph 2-A. If he or she makes 0-2 mistakes, then the student can read material at this level independently, too. Check "Independent."

The student next reads Paragraph 2-B. If three to four mistakes are made, you have found the Instructional Reading Level. Check "Instructional" to the right of that paragraph. This is the level at which reading instruction will be most effective for that student.

Notice that the number of mistakes for each reading level is shown on the test to the right of the paragraph. The number of mistakes varies. In Paragraphs 1-A through 2-B, three to four mistakes yield a student's Instructional Reading Level; in Paragraphs 3-A and 3-B, two to three mistakes give the Instructional Reading Level; and in Paragraphs 4 through 7 only two mistakes do so.

After finding the student's Instructional Reading Level, continue the test until you find the Frustration Reading Level. In Paragraphs 3-A and 3-B, four or more mistakes in a single paragraph indicate a student's Frustration Reading Level. In Paragraphs 4 through 7, three or more mistakes show the Frustration Reading Level. Stop testing when you get to the student's Frustration Level.

Record the results of the test in the spaces provided on the first page of the test. Fill in the highest grade level of material that the student can handle independently. Then record the grade level of material that should be used with him or her for instruction.

Do not use this test for instruction. If a student misses a word, tell him or her to "go on." Do not supply any hints or tell the word. If this policy is followed, the same test can be used later to determine progress. When retesting a student, use different color pencils to underline mistakes. Spaces have been provided for recording results of retests. Keep the record sheet for easy reference and for retesting.

Speed

The paragraphs are not timed, but excessive rapidity or slowness may be noted to the right of the paragraph as an important characteristic of the student's reading ability. Slow reading means more practice is needed at that level so the student can gain fluency.

Grade Levels of the Paragraphs

There are two paragraphs per grade level for grades one through three. The first paragraph is marked 1-A. This means "easy first grade." The next is marked 1-B. This means "hard first grade." There is only one paragraph for each level beyond third.

The last paragraph is marked grade seven, but actually it is indicative of popular adult and non-academic or non-technical secondary reading levels. If a student can read it perfectly, he or she can do most junior and senior high school readings satisfactorily. For a more accurate determination of reading ability for students reading at junior and senior high school levels, a standardized silent reading test is recommended.

Comprehension

The Oral Reading Test does not measure comprehension. For most elementary reading levels, it is fairly safe to assume that comprehension roughly equals oral reading ability, but certainly comprehension is a skill well worth measuring.

The Silent Reading Comprehension Tests located on pages 96 through 107 and discussed in the Step 3 chapter will help you assess your students' silent reading comprehension.

Oral Reading Test: Student Copy

Directions: Have the student read from this copy.

No. 1-A

Look at the dog.

It is big.

It can run.

Run, dog, run away.

No. 1-B

We saw the sun.

It made us warm.

Now it was time to go home.

It was a long way to walk.

No. 2-A

The door of the house opened, and a man came out.
He had a broom in his hand. He said to the boy sitting
there, "Go away." The boy got up and left.

No. 2-B

The family ate their breakfast. Then they gave the pig
his breakfast. It was fun to watch him eat. He seemed
to like it. He was eating all of it.

Oral Reading Test: Student Copy *(cont.)*

No. 3-A

When the man had gone, the boys were surprised to see how many boxes he had left in their little backyard. Right away they began to pile them on top of each other. It took so long that lunch time came before they knew they were hungry.

No. 3-B

The man became angry because his dog had never talked before, and, besides, he didn't like its voice. So he took his knife and cut a branch from a palm tree and hit his dog. Just then the palm tree said, "Put down that branch." The man was getting very upset about the way things were going, and he started to throw it away.

No. 4

Three more cowboys tried their best to rope and tie a calf as quickly as Red, but none of them came within ten seconds of his time. Then came the long, thin cowboy. He was the last one to enter the contest.

Oral Reading Test: Student Copy *(cont.)*

No. 5

High in the hills, they came to a wide ledge where trees grew among
the rocks. Grass grew in patches, and the ground was covered with
bits of wood from trees blown over a long time ago and dried by the
sun. Down in the valley, it was already beginning to get dark.

No. 6

Businessmen from suburban areas may travel to work in helicopters,
land on the roof of an office building, and thus avoid city traffic jams.
Families can spend more time at summer homes and mountain cabins
through the use of this marvelous craft. People on farms can reach
city centers quickly for medical service, shopping, entertainment, or
sale of products.

No. 7

The President of the United States was speaking. His audience was
comprised of two thousand foreign-born men and women who had
just been admitted to citizenship. They listened intently, their faces
aglow with the light of a newborn patriotism, upturned to the calm,
intellectual face of the first citizen of the country they now claimed as
their own.

Oral Reading Test
Examiner's Copy and Record Sheet
for Determining Independent and Instructional Reading Levels

Student's Name _____ Date _____

Examiner _____ Class _____

	1st Testing	2nd Testing	3rd Testing
Date	_____	_____	_____
Total Score: Independent Reading Level	Grade	Grade	Grade
	_____	_____	_____
Independent Reading Level	Grade	Grade	Grade
	_____	_____	_____

Directions: The student reads aloud from the student copy—**not** this copy. If the student cannot read a word or mispronounces it, say, "Go on," and count it as an error (underline the word). Do **not** tell the student the missed word. Stop the test when the Frustration Level is first reached.

No. 1-A (Easy First Grade)

Look at the dog.

It is big.

It can run.

Run, dog, run away.

Errors	Level	1st Testing	2nd Testing	3rd Testing
0–2	Independent	☐	☐	☐
3–4	Instructional	☐	☐	☐
5+	Frustration	☐	☐	☐
Fluency:	Excellent	☐	☐	☐
	Good	☐	☐	☐
	Poor	☐	☐	☐
	Very Poor	☐	☐	☐

No. 1-B (Hard First Grade)

We saw the sun.

It made us warm.

Now it was time to go home.

It was a long way to walk.

Errors	Level	1st Testing	2nd Testing	3rd Testing
0–2	Independent	☐	☐	☐
3–4	Instructional	☐	☐	☐
5+	Frustration	☐	☐	☐
Fluency:	Excellent	☐	☐	☐
	Good	☐	☐	☐
	Poor	☐	☐	☐
	Very Poor	☐	☐	☐

Oral Reading Test *(cont.)*
Examiner's Copy and Record Sheet
for Determining Independent and Instructional Reading Levels

		1st Testing	2nd Testing	3rd Testing

No. 2-A (Easy Second Grade)

The door of the house opened, and a man came out. He had a broom in his hand. He said to the boy sitting there, "Go away." The boy got up and left.

Errors	Level	1st Testing	2nd Testing	3rd Testing
0–2	Independent	☐	☐	☐
3–4	Instructional	☐	☐	☐
5+	Frustration	☐	☐	☐
Fluency:	Excellent	☐	☐	☐
	Good	☐	☐	☐
	Poor	☐	☐	☐
	Very Poor	☐	☐	☐

No. 2-B (Hard Second Grade)

The family ate their breakfast. Then they gave the pig his breakfast. It was fun to watch him eat. He seemed to like it. He was eating all of it.

Errors	Level	1st Testing	2nd Testing	3rd Testing
0–2	Independent	☐	☐	☐
3–4	Instructional	☐	☐	☐
5+	Frustration	☐	☐	☐
Fluency:	Excellent	☐	☐	☐
	Good	☐	☐	☐
	Poor	☐	☐	☐
	Very Poor	☐	☐	☐

No. 3-A (Easy Third Grade)

When the man had gone, the boys were surprised to see how many boxes he had left in their little backyard. Right away they began to pile them on top of each other. It took so long that lunch time came before they knew they were hungry.

Errors	Level	1st Testing	2nd Testing	3rd Testing
0–1	Independent	☐	☐	☐
2–3	Instructional	☐	☐	☐
4+	Frustration	☐	☐	☐
Fluency:	Excellent	☐	☐	☐
	Good	☐	☐	☐
	Poor	☐	☐	☐
	Very Poor	☐	☐	☐

Oral Reading Test *(cont.)*
Examiner's Copy and Record Sheet
for Determining Independent and Instructional Reading Levels

No. 3-B (Hard Third Grade)

The man became angry because his dog had never talked before, and, besides, he didn't like its voice. So he took his knife and cut a branch from a palm tree and hit his dog. Just then the palm tree said, "Put down that branch." The man was getting very upset about the way things were going, and he started to throw it away.

		1st Testing	2nd Testing	3rd Testing
Errors	**Level**			
0–1	Independent	☐	☐	☐
2–3	Instructional	☐	☐	☐
4+	Frustration	☐	☐	☐
Fluency:	Excellent	☐	☐	☐
	Good	☐	☐	☐
	Poor	☐	☐	☐
	Very Poor	☐	☐	☐

No. 4 (Fourth Grade)

Three more cowboys tried their best to rope and tie a calf as quickly as Red, but none of them came within ten seconds of his time. Then came the long, thin cowboy. He was the last one to enter the contest.

		1st Testing	2nd Testing	3rd Testing
Errors	**Level**			
0–1	Independent	☐	☐	☐
2	Instructional	☐	☐	☐
3+	Frustration	☐	☐	☐
Fluency:	Excellent	☐	☐	☐
	Good	☐	☐	☐
	Poor	☐	☐	☐
	Very Poor	☐	☐	☐

No. 5 (Fifth Grade)

High in the hills, they came to a wide ledge where trees grew among the rocks. Grass grew in patches, and the ground was covered with bits of wood from trees blown over a long time ago and dried by the sun. Down in the valley, it was already beginning to get dark.

		1st Testing	2nd Testing	3rd Testing
Errors	**Level**			
0–1	Independent	☐	☐	☐
2	Instructional	☐	☐	☐
3+	Frustration	☐	☐	☐
Fluency:	Excellent	☐	☐	☐
	Good	☐	☐	☐
	Poor	☐	☐	☐
	Very Poor	☐	☐	☐

Oral Reading Test *(cont.)*
Examiner's Copy and Record Sheet
for Determining Independent and Instructional Reading Levels

		1st Testing	2nd Testing	3rd Testing

No. 6 (Sixth Grade)

Businessmen from suburban areas may travel to work in helicopters, land on the roof of an office building, and thus avoid city traffic jams. Families can spend more time at summer homes and mountain cabins through the use of this marvelous craft. People on farms can reach city centers quickly for medical service, shopping, entertainment, or sale of products.

Errors	Level	1st Testing	2nd Testing	3rd Testing
0–1	Independent	☐	☐	☐
2	Instructional	☐	☐	☐
3+	Frustration	☐	☐	☐
Fluency:	Excellent	☐	☐	☐
	Good	☐	☐	☐
	Poor	☐	☐	☐
	Very Poor	☐	☐	☐

No. 7 (Seventh Grade)

The President of the United States was speaking. His audience was comprised of two thousand foreign-born men and women who had just been admitted to citizenship. They listened intently, their faces aglow with the light of a newborn patriotism, upturned to the calm, intellectual face of the first citizen of the country they now claimed as their own.

Errors	Level	1st Testing	2nd Testing	3rd Testing
0–1	Independent	☐	☐	☐
2	Instructional	☐	☐	☐
3+	Frustration	☐	☐	☐
Fluency:	Excellent	☐	☐	☐
	Good	☐	☐	☐
	Poor	☐	☐	☐
	Very Poor	☐	☐	☐

NOTE: If the last paragraph is read at the Independent Level, use a silent reading test to determine advanced skills.

Interest Inventory for Children

Directions: Have the student fill this out—with teacher assistance, if necessary. Use this information to select interesting stories and reading materials. Most of these items can also be used as story starters or titles for students' themes.

My name is _____ .

I am _____ **years old.**

Outside of school, the thing I like to do best is_____ .

In school, the thing I like best is_____ .

If I had a million dollars, I would _____ .

When I grow up, I will_____ .

I hate _____ .

My favorite animal is_____ .

The best sport is_____ .

When nobody is around, I like to_____ .

The person I like best is _____ .

Next summer I hope to _____ .

My father's work is _____ .

My mother's work is _____ .

When I grow up, I will be _____ .

I like to collect _____ .

The things I like to make are _____ .

My favorite place to be is _____ .

The best book I ever read was _____ .

The best TV show is_____ .

My favorite school subjects are _____ .

Interest Inventory for Adults

Directions: Have the student fill this out—with teacher assistance, if necessary. Use this information to select interesting stories and reading materials. Most of these items can also be used as story starters or titles for students' themes.

Name _____

Occupation _____

Describe briefly what you do. _____

What do you need to read on the job? _____

What would you like to read for pleasure? _____

What is your hobby? _____

What sport are you interested in?_____

What would you do if you won a million dollars?_____

What kind of further schooling might you do?_____

What books have you read?_____

What do you do on vacation? _____

Have you ever had your eyes and hearing checked?_____

What kind of work would you like to do in the future? _____

If you moved, where would you like to go? _____

What are your favorite kinds of food and drink? _____

What is your favorite TV show? _____

Grade-Level Book List: Gunning

Level 1.0–1.1
Brown Bear, Brown Bear, What Do You See? by Bill Martin
Bugs by Patricia and Frederick McKissack
Who Is Who? by Patricia McKissack

Level 1.2–1.3
The Ant and the Dove by Mary Lewis Want
The Foot Book by Dr. Seuss
Sleepy Dog by Harriet Ziefert

Level 1.4–1.5
And I Mean It, Stanley! by Crosby Bonsall
Jason's Bus Ride by Harriet Ziefert
The Cake That Mack Ate by Rose Robart

Level 1.6–1.7
Little Bear's Visit by Else Minark
Clifford, the Small Red Puppy by Norman Bridwell
You Hoo, Moon! by William Hooks

Level 1.8–1.9
Henry and Mudge: The First Book by Cynthia Rylant
Frog and Toad at Home by Arnold Lobel
Feed Me by William Hooks

Level 2.0–2.5
Bread and Jam for Frances by Russell Hoban
Thank You, Amelia Bedelia by Peggy Parish
Stone Soup by Ann McGovern

Gunning, Thomas G. *Best Books for Beginning Readers.* Boston, MA:
Allyn and Bacon, 1998.

Grade-Level Book List: Pinnell and Fountas

Level	Title	Author
K-1	*I Can Read*	Ready to Read
1-2	*Goodnight Moon*	Margaret Wise Brown
2	*Green Eggs and Ham*	Dr. Seuss
2	*Cat in the Hat*	Dr. Seuss
2	*Henry and Mudge: The First Book*	Cynthia Rylant
2	*Madeline*	Ludwig Bemelmaus
2-3	*Amelia Bedelia*	Peggy Parish
2-3	*Sea Otters*	Storytellers Nonfiction
2-3	*Tale of Peter Rabbit*	Beatrix Potter
2-3	*Rats on the Roof*	James Marshall
3	*Say Hola, Sara*	Patricia Reilly Giff
3-4	*Henry Huggins*	Beverly Cleary
3-4	*Magic School Bus Blows Its Top*	Joanna Cole
3-4	*Mr. Popper's Penguins*	Richard and Florence Atwater
4	*Encyclopedia Brown, Boy Detective*	Donald and Rose Sobol
4	*Berenstain Bear Scouts*	Stan and Jan Berenstain

Fountas, Irene C. and Gay Su Pinnell. *Matching Books to Readers: Using Leveled Books in Guided Reading*. Portsmouth, NH: Heinemann, 1999.

Silent Reading Comprehension Tests

Administering the Test

If the test is to be administered to a group, make copies of the test for the appropriate level and give each student a copy. (If only one student is taking the test, he or she may use the test in the manual and write the answers on a separate sheet of paper.) Read the directions below with the students and then tell them to begin:

Read the stories and questions about the stories. You are to read each story carefully and then fill in the spaces next to the best answer to the question. You may look back at a story if it helps you answer the question. Don't rush, but don't waste time either.

Scoring and Interpretation

These two Silent Reading Comprehension Tests are designed to give you a general idea of a student's comprehension ability in a short period of time. They are shorter than most regular comprehension tests and, hence, not quite as precise. However, they are a good supplement to a teacher's subjective opinion.

You can tell how your student compares with typical third graders on Test A (pages 98-101) and with typical seventh graders on Test B (pages 102-107). It doesn't make any difference what age or grade your student happens to be.

The Answer Key on the next page tells you the type of comprehension tested (vocabulary, main idea, inference, and so on) for each item, as well as the percentage of students passing the item at grade level three or seven. This gives you some idea of the item difficulty and the kinds of abilities in which your student may be strong or weak.

A total score (total number of items correct) also gives a more general notion of your students' reading comprehension abilities. A total score of eight correct on Test A would be average for nine-year-olds who would most likely be in mid-third grade. A total score of seven on Test B would be average for 13-year-olds who would most likely be in mid-seventh grade. You can see how your students do in comparison with these guideposts.

Reading comprehension improves with teaching, so teach it for awhile, using the ideas in Step 3 and in the list of reading materials. Then retest your students, using the Silent Reading Comprehension Tests to see if they have improved.

Answer Key

Test A is intended for nine-year-olds, third grade. A score of eight correct is average for nine-year-olds, who would most likely be in mid-third grade. It indicates average third-grade reading ability.

Item	Answer	Question Type	Percentage of Success for Nine-Year-Olds (National Norms)
1	b	Vocabulary	92%
2	d	Reference	63%
3	d	Facts	86%
4	d	Organization	83%
5	e	Main Idea	84%
6	c	Inferences	75%
7	b	Inferences	86%
8	c	Inferences	60%
9	c	Critical Reading	75%
10	a	Critical Reading	75%

Test B is intended for 13-year-olds, seventh grade. A score of seven correct is average for 13-year-olds, who would most likely be in mid-seventh grade. It indicates average seventh-grade reading ability.

Item	Answer	Question Type	Percentage of Success for 13-Year-Olds (National Norms)
1	b	Vocabulary	76%
2	c	Reference	74%
3	a	Facts	68%
4	d	Organization	90%
5	c	Main Idea	88%
6	b	Inferences	86%
7	e	Inferences	72%
8	e	Inferences	55%
9	b	Critical Reading	56%
10	b	Critical Reading	50%

In each test, the first five questions are literal type questions and the second five are inferential type questions.

Silent Reading Comprehension Test A
Student's Copy

Name _____ Grade _____ Date _____

Directions: Read the stories and questions about the stories. You are to read each story carefully and then fill in the space next to the best answer to the question. You may look back at a story if it helps you answer the question. Don't rush, but don't waste time, either.

1. Read the sentences and do what they tell you to do.

   ☐ a. **If you have ever visited the moon, fill in the box here.**

   ☐ b. **If you have never visited the moon, fill in the box here.**

2. You want to call Mr. Jones on the telephone. You look in the telephone book for his number. You would find it between which names?

   ☐ a. **Jackson and Jacobs**

   ☐ b. **Jacobs and James**

   ☐ c. **James and Johnson**

   ☐ d. **Johnson and Judson**

   ☐ e. **Judson and Justus**

   ☐ f. **I don't know.**

3. Read the story and complete the sentence that follows it.

   The wind pushed the boat farther and farther out to sea. It started to rain, and the fog grew thick. The boy and his father were lost at sea.

   The weather was

   ☐ a. **calm.**

   ☐ b. **dry.**

   ☐ c. **sunny.**

   ☐ d. **wet.**

   ☐ e. **I don't know.**

4. Read the story and answer the question which follows it.

The wind pushed the boat farther and farther out to sea. It started to rain, and the fog grew thick. The boy and his father were lost at sea.

What happened first in the story?
- ☐ a. **It became foggy.**
- ☐ b. **It started to rain.**
- ☐ c. **The boat turned over.**
- ☐ d. **The boat went out to sea.**
- ☐ e. **I don't know.**

5. Read the passage and answer the question which follows it.

A sports car differs from an ordinary passenger car in that its size and number of accessories are limited. The sports car also differs from the ordinary passenger car in performance. It can attain higher speeds because it is built smaller and lower. For these reasons it can also turn corners faster and more smoothly than a passenger car. Also a sports car generally gets better gas mileage than an ordinary passenger car.

What does the writer tell you about sports cars?
- ☐ a. **Prices**
- ☐ b. **Colors and styles**
- ☐ c. **Places to buy them**
- ☐ d. **Number of people they hold**
- ☐ e. **How sports cars differ from passenger cars**
- ☐ f. **I don't know.**

6. This is like a game to see if you can tell what the nonsense word in the paragraph stands for. The nonsense word is just a silly word for something that you know very well. Read the paragraph and see if you can tell what the underlined nonsense word stand for.

Most people have two <u>cags</u>. You use your <u>cags</u> to hold things when you eat or brush your teeth. Some people write with their left <u>cag</u>, and some people write with their right <u>cag</u>.

Cags are probably

- ☐ a. **eyes.**
- ☐ b. **feet.**
- ☐ c. **hands.**
- ☐ d. **pencils.**
- ☐ e. **I don't know.**

7. Read the story and answer the question that follows it.

The wind pushed the boat farther and farther out to sea. It started to rain, and the fog grew thick. The boy and his father were lost at sea.

At least how many people were in the boat?

- ☐ a. **one**
- ☐ b. **two**
- ☐ c. **three**
- ☐ d. **four**
- ☐ e. **five**
- ☐ f. **I don't know.**

8. Read the story and answer the question that follows it.

Christmas was only a few days away. The wind was strong and cold. The sidewalks were covered with snow. The downtown streets were crowded with people. Their faces were hidden by many packages as they went in one store after another. They all tried to move faster as they looked at the clock.

When did the story probably happen?

- ☐ a. **November 28**
- ☐ b. **December 1**
- ☐ c. **December 21**
- ☐ d. **December 25**
- ☐ e. **December 28**
- ☐ f. **I don't know.**

9. Read the story about a fish and answer the question that follows it.

   Once there was a fish named Big Eyes who was tired of swimming. He wanted to get out of the water and walk like other animals do, so one day, without telling anyone, he just jumped out of the water, put on his shoes, and took a long walk around the park.

   What do you think the person who wrote this story was trying to do?

   ☐ a. **Tell you what fish are like**
   ☐ b. **Tell you that fish wear shoes**
   ☐ c. **Tell you a funny story about a fish**
   ☐ d. **Tell you that fish don't like to swim**
   ☐ e. **I don't know.**

10. If you listen carefully to what a person says, you can usually tell a lot about him or her. Sometimes you can tell how that person feels.

    Read the passage and complete the sentence that follows it.

    "I'll be glad when this TV show is over. I like stories about spies, not this one about cowboys and Indians. I get to pick the next show."

    The person who said this

    ☐ a. **likes spy stories.**
    ☐ b. **doesn't like TV at all.**
    ☐ c. **doesn't care what TV show is on.**
    ☐ d. **likes stories about cowboys and Indians.**
    ☐ e. **I don't know.**

Silent Reading Comprehension Test B

Student's Copy

Name _____ Grade _____ Date _____

Directions: Below are a number of stories and questions about the stories. You are to read each story carefully and then fill in the space next to the best answer to the question. You may look back at a story if it helps you answer the question. Don't rush, but don't waste time, either.

1. Read the sentence and fill in the box beside the group of words which tells what the sentence means.

   "I *certainly* won't miss that movie."

   ☐ a. **I like that movie.**

   ☐ b. **I'm going to that movie.**

   ☐ c. **I'm not going to that movie.**

   ☐ d. **I hope I'll see that movie, but I don't know if I can.**

   ☐ e. **I didn't see that movie, although it was here all fall.**

   ☐ f. **I don't know.**

2. Read the directions from a can of insecticide spray and answer the question which follows them.

   ### *ABC Bug Spray*

   **Kills: spiders, roaches, ants, and most other crawling insects.
   Directions: Spray surfaces over which insects may crawl: doorways, window ledges, cracks, etc. Hold can approximately 10 inches from surface. Do not use near uncovered food or small children.
   Toxic.**

Which of the following will probably not be killed by the spray?

☐ a. **Ants**

☐ b. **Caterpillars**

☐ c. **Flies**

☐ d. **Roaches**

☐ e. **Spiders**

☐ f. **I don't know.**

3. What is the best way to find out if there is something about Eskimos in a book?

☐ a. **Look in the index.**

☐ b. **Look in the glossary.**

☐ c. **Look at the title page.**

☐ d. **Look through all the pages.**

☐ e. **Skim through the introduction.**

☐ f. **I don't know.**

4. Read the passage and answer the question which follows it.

It should come as no surprise to learn that 9 out of 10 Americans are in debt. In fact, 5 out of 10 are heavily in debt. How heavily is borne out by government statistics that show that income has increased 50% while debts have increased 110%!

Putting statistics into their proper perspective: paying off the car, the home, the groceries, the doctors, and even the children's education is now a way of life for over a hundred million Americans. Very few of us could get by if we had to pay cash when we buy. Keeping up with the Joneses is made easier for us by easy payment plans, easy-to-acquire charge cards, and easy-to-borrow bank loans.

According to the article, how many Americans are in debt?

☐ a. **50%**　　　　☐ d. **9 out of 10**

☐ b. **2 out of 3**　　☐ e. **I don't know.**

☐ c. **4 out of 5**

5. Read the two stories and answer the question which follows them.

Story 1

A handsome prince was riding his horse in the woods. He saw a dragon chasing a beautiful princess. The prince killed the dragon. The prince and the princess were then married.

Story 2

Mary was taking a boat ride on a lake. The boat tipped over. Mary was about to drown when a young man jumped in the lake and saved her.

If Story 2 ends like Story 1, what would happen next in Story 2?

☐ a. **A prince would kill a dragon.**

☐ b. **The young man would become a prince.**

☐ c. **Mary and the young man would get married.**

☐ d. **The king would give the young man some money.**

☐ e. **I don't know.**

6. Read the story and answer the question which follows it.

Sammy got to school ten minutes after the school bell had rung. He was breathing hard and had a black eye. His face was dirty and scratched. One leg of his pants was torn.

Tommy was late to school, too; however, he was only five minutes late. Like Sammy, he was breathing hard, but he was happy and smiling.

Sammy and Tommy had been fighting.

Who probably won?

☐ a. **Sammy**   ☐ c. **Cannot tell from the story**

☐ b. **Tommy**   ☐ d. **I don't know.**

7. Read the passage and answer the question which follows it.

One spring, Farmer Brown had an unusually good field of wheat. Whenever he saw any birds in this field, he got his gun and shot as many of them as he could.

In the middle of the summer he found that the insects had multiplied very fast. What Farmer Brown did not understand was this: A bird is not simply an animal that eats food the farmer may want for himself. Instead, it is one of many links in the complex surroundings, or environment, in which we live.

How much grain a farmer can raise on an acre of ground depends on many factors. All of these factors can be divided into two big groups. Such things as the richness of the soil, the amount of rainfall, the amount of sunlight, and the temperature belong together in one of the groups. This group may be called _living factors_. The living factors in any plant's environment are animals and other plants. Wheat, for example, may be damaged by wheat rust, a tiny plant that feeds on wheat; or it may be eaten by plant-eating animals such as birds or grasshoppers.

It is easy to see that the relationship of plants and animals to their environment is very complex and that any change in the environment is likely to bring about a whole series of changes.

What important idea about nature does the writer want us to understand?

☐ a. **Farmer Brown was worried about the heavy rainfall.**

☐ b. **Nobody needs to have such destructive birds around.**

☐ c. **Farmer Brown didn't want the temperature to change.**

☐ d. **All insects need not only wheat rust but grasshoppers.**

☐ e. **All living things are dependent on other living things.**

☐ f. **I don't know.**

8. Read the passage and complete the sentence that follows it.

   Art says that the polar ice cap is melting at the rate of 3% per year. Bert says that this isn't true because the polar ice cap is really melting at the rate of 7% per year.

   We know for certain that
   - ☐ a. **Art is wrong.**
   - ☐ b. **Bert is wrong.**
   - ☐ c. **They are both wrong.**
   - ☐ d. **They both might be right.**
   - ☐ e. **They can't both be right.**
   - ☐ f. **I don't know.**

9. Read the passage and answer the question that follows it.

   Johnny told Billy that he could make it rain any time he wanted to by stepping on a spider. Billy said he couldn't. Johnny stepped on a spider. That night it rained. The next day Johnny told Billy, "That proves I can make it rain any time I want to."

   Was Johnny right?
   - ☐ a. **Yes**
   - ☐ b. **No**
   - ☐ c. **Can't tell from the passage**
   - ☐ d. **I don't know.**

10. Read the poem and answer the question that follows it.

> **My body a rounded stone**
> **With a pattern of smooth seams,**
> **My head a short snake,**
> **Retractive, protective.**
> **My legs come out of their sleeves**
> **Or shrink within,**
> **And so does my chin.**
> **My eyelids are quick clamps.**
> **My back is my roof.**
> **I am always at home.**
> **I travel where my house walks.**
> **It is a smooth stone.**
> **It floats within the lake,**
> **Or rests in the dust.**
> **My flesh lives tenderly**
> **Inside its home.**

Which word best describes the speaker in the poem?

☐ a. **confused**   ☐ d. **restless**

☐ b. **contented**   ☐ e. **unhappy**

☐ c. **excited**   ☐ f. **I don't know.**

600 Instant Words

These are the most often used words in reading and writing. The first 100 words are listed in order of frequency in Columns 1 through 4. Make sure your student knows most of these before teaching the second 100. Teach only a few words at a time to keep the success rate high. Use these words for flash cards, games, spelling lessons, or just read down the column. These high frequency words are also called "sight words" because they must be recognized instantly, on sight, for reading fluency.

Words 1–25	Words 26–50	Words 51–75	Words 76–100
the	or	will	number
of	one	up	no
and	had	other	way
a	by	about	could
to	words	out	people
in	but	many	my
is	not	then	than
you	what	them	first
that	all	these	water
it	were	so	been
he	we	some	called
was	when	her	who
for	your	would	am
on	can	make	its
are	said	like	now
as	there	him	find
with	use	into	long
his	an	time	down
they	each	has	day
I	which	look	did
at	she	two	get
be	do	more	come
this	how	write	made
have	their	go	may
from	if	see	part

600 Instant Words *(cont.)*

The Second 100 Instant Words

Words 101–125	Words 126–150	Words 151–175	Words 176–200
over	say	set	try
new	great	put	kind
sound	where	end	hand
take	help	does	picture
only	through	another	again
little	much	well	change
work	before	large	off
know	line	must	play
place	right	big	spell
years	too	even	air
live	means	such	away
me	old	because	animals
back	any	turned	house
give	same	here	point
most	tell	why	page
very	boy	asked	letters
after	following	went	mother
things	came	men	answer
our	want	read	found
just	show	need	study
name	also	land	still
good	around	different	learn
sentence	farm	home	should
man	three	us	American
think	small	move	world

600 Instant Words *(cont.)*

The Third 100 Instant Words

Words 201–225	Words 226–250	Words 251–275	Words 276–300
high	saw	important	miss
every	left	until	idea
near	don't	children	enough
add	few	side	eat
food	while	feet	face
between	along	car	watch
own	might	miles	far
below	close	night	Indians
country	something	walked	really
plants	seemed	white	almost
last	next	sea	let
school	hard	began	above
father	open	grow	girl
keep	example	took	sometimes
trees	beginning	river	mountains
never	life	four	cut
started	always	carry	young
city	those	state	talk
earth	both	once	soon
eyes	paper	book	list
light	together	hear	song
thought	got	stop	being
head	group	without	leave
under	often	second	family
story	run	later	it's

600 Instant Words *(cont.)*

The Fourth 100 Instant Words

Words 301–325	Words 326–350	Words 351–375	Words 376–400
body	order	listen	busy
music	red	wind	pulled
color	door	rock	draw
stand	sure	space	voice
sun	become	covered	seen
questions	top	fast	cold
fish	ship	several	cried
area	across	hold	plan
mark	today	himself	notice
dog	during	toward	south
horse	short	five	sing
birds	better	step	war
problem	best	morning	ground
complete	however	passed	fall
room	low	vowel	king
knew	hours	true	town
since	black	hundred	I'll
ever	products	against	unit
piece	happened	pattern	figure
told	whole	numeral	certain
usually	measure	table	field
didn't	remember	north	travel
friends	early	slowly	wood
easy	waves	money	fire
heard	reached	map	upon

600 Instant Words *(cont.)*

The Fifth 100 Instant Words

Words 401–425	Words 426–450	Words 451–475	Words 476–500
done	decided	plane	filled
English	contain	system	heat
road	course	behind	full
half	surface	ran	hot
ten	produce	round	check
fly	building	boat	object
gave	ocean	game	bread
box	class	force	rule
finally	note	brought	among
wait	nothing	understand	noun
correct	rest	warm	power
oh	carefully	common	cannot
quickly	scientists	bring	able
person	inside	explain	six
became	wheels	dry	size
shown	stay	though	dark
minutes	green	language	ball
strong	known	shape	material
verb	island	deep	special
stars	week	thousands	heavy
front	less	yes	fine
feel	machine	clear	pair
fact	base	equation	circle
inches	ago	yet	include
street	stood	government	built

600 Instant Words *(cont.)*

The Sixth 100 Instant Words

Words 501–525	Words 526–550	Words 551–575	Words 576–600
can't	picked	legs	beside
matter	simple	sat	gone
square	cells	main	sky
syllables	paint	winter	glass
perhaps	mind	wide	million
bill	love	written	west
felt	cause	length	lay
suddenly	rain	reason	weather
test	exercise	kept	root
direction	eggs	interest	instruments
center	train	arms	meet
farmers	blue	brother	third
ready	wish	race	months
anything	drop	present	paragraph
divided	developed	beautiful	raised
general	window	store	represent
energy	difference	job	soft
subject	distance	edge	whether
Europe	heart	past	clothes
moon	sit	sign	flowers
region	sum	record	shall
return	summer	finished	teacher
believe	wall	discovered	held
dance	forest	wild	describe
members	probably	happy	drive

NOTE: The entire list of 3,000 Instant Words can be found in *Spelling Book, Words Most Needed Plus Phonics for Grades 1–6* (TCM 1750), available from Teacher Created Materials.

Instant Words Test: Directions

The Instant Words Test is located on the next page. Ask the pupil to read each word aloud slowly. The examiner should use a copy of the Instant Word Test for scoring. Place a "C" next to each word read correctly. Although you should allow for regional dialect differences, accept only proper pronunciations. Do not give any aid. If a pupil does not know a word, tell him or her to go on to the next word after five seconds.

Discontinue when the student misses five words, not necessarily in consecutive order. Find the last correct word before the fifth error, and multiply its position number by 15. This will give you the student's *approximate* instructional placement.

Because it is not standardized, the test does not yield a grade level score, but it can be used to determine where to begin working with a student on the 600 Instant Words. Do not use this test for teaching; use the complete list of 600 Instant Words, which starts on page 108.

Instant Words Test

Student's Name _____

Examiner _____

Date_____ Class _____

Test for the First 300 Words
(approximately every 15th word in the first 300 words)

1. are
2. but
3. which
4. so
5. see
6. now
7. only
8. just
9. too
10. small
11. why
12. again
13. study
14. last
15. story
16. beginning
17. feet
18. book
19. almost
20. family

Test for the Second 300 Words
(approximately every 15th word in the second 300 words)

21. room
22. become
23. whole
24. toward
25. map
26. king
27. certain
28. stars
29. nothing
30. stood
31. bring
32. check
33. heavy
34. direction
35. picked
36. window
37. wide
38. sign
39. root
40. describe

Directions: The student reads aloud from one copy; the examiner marks another copy. Stop after the student misses any five words. Do not help the student. If the student makes an error or hesitates five seconds, say, "Try the next word."

Scoring:

( ) Position number of last correct word before the fifth word missed
X 15

( ) Approximate placement on the 600 Instant Words

For example, if the last correct word was 10, then 10 x 15 = 150. So start teaching the Instant Words with word 151 in column 7.

100 Picture Nouns

These words are intended to supplement the first 300 Instant Words for use in beginning or remedial reading instruction. These words can be made into flash cards with the word on one side only or cards with the word on one side and a picture on the other.

front	back
dog	

1. PEOPLE
   boy
   girl
   man
   woman
   baby

2. TOYS
   ball
   doll
   train
   game
   toy

3. NUMBERS 1–5
   one
   two
   three
   four
   five

4. CLOTHING
   shirt
   pants
   dress
   shoes
   hat

5. PETS
   cat
   dog
   bird
   fish
   rabbit

6. FURNITURE
   table
   chair
   sofa
   chest
   desk

7. EATING OBJECTS
   cup
   plate
   bowl
   fork
   spoon

8. TRANSPORTATION
   car
   truck
   bus
   plane
   boat

9. FOOD
   bread
   meat
   soup
   apple
   cereal

10. DRINKS
    water
    milk
    juice
    soda
    malt

100 Picture Nouns *(cont.)*

11. NUMBERS 6–10
    six
    seven
    eight
    nine
    ten

12. FRUIT
    fruit
    orange
    grape
    pear
    banana

13. PLANTS
    bush
    flower
    grass
    plant
    tree

14. SKY THINGS
    sun
    moon
    star
    cloud
    rain

15. EARTH THINGS
    lake
    rock
    dirt
    field
    hill

16. FARM ANIMALS
    horse
    cow
    pig
    chicken
    duck

17. WORKERS
    farmer
    policeman
    cook
    doctor
    nurse

18. ENTERTAINMENT
    television
    radio
    movie
    ball game
    band

19. WRITING TOOLS
    pen
    pencil
    crayon
    chalk
    computer

20. READING THINGS
    book
    newspaper
    magazine
    sign
    letter

Prefixes

Prefix	Meaning	Example
anti-	against	antiwar, antinuclear, antisocial, antislavery
auto-	self	automobile, automatic, autograph, autobiography
bi-, bin-	two	bicycle, binocular, biceps, bifocal, biplane
cent-	hundred	centigrade, century, cent, centimeter
de-	opposite	deactivate, deform, degrade
dis-	opposite	disagree, dishonest, discontinue
im-	into	import, implant, immigrate
im-	not	imbalance, impossible, immature
inter-	among, between	interrupt, intermission, international, interpret, intervene
micro-	small, short	microphone, microscope, microbe, microfilm
mid-	middle	midnight, midsummer, midway, midyear

Prefixes *(cont.)*

Prefix	Meaning	Example
mis-	bad	misbehavior, misconduct, misfortune
non-	not	nonsense, noncomform, nondescript
over-	too much	overactive, overpriced, overdo
pre-	before	prefix, prejudice, precaution
re-	again	redo, rewrite, reappear, repaint, relive
semi-	half	semiannual, semicircle, semiconscious
sub-	under	submarine, subordinate, subterranean
super-	more than	superhuman, supernatural, superpower, superfine
tele-	distant	telephone, telescope, telegram, television
trans-	across	transatlantic, transcend, transfer, translate
tri-	three	triangle, tricycle, trillion, triplet
un-	not	unhappy, unable, unbeaten, uncertain, uncomfortable
under-	below	underneath, undercover, underground, underpass

Greek Roots

Root	Meaning	Examples
aero	air	aerospace, aeronautics, aerosol, aeroplane (alternate spelling of airplane)
ast	star	astronaut, astronomy, asteroid, asterisk
cycl	circle, ring	bicycle, cyclone, cycle, encyclopedia, cyclops
gram	letter, written	telegram, diagram, grammar, epigram, monogram
graph	write	telegraph, photograph, phonograph, autograph
meter	measure	thermometer, centimeter, diameter, barometer
phon	sound	phonograph, symphony, telephone, microphone, phonics
photo	light	photograph, photography, telephoto, photosynthesis
pop	people	population, popular, populace
scop	see	microscope, telescope, periscope, stethoscope
therm	heat	thermometer, thermal, thermostat, thermos

Latin Roots

Root	Meaning	Examples
act	do	action, react, transact, actor, enact
ang	bend	angle, triangle, quadrangle, angular
aud	hear	auditorium, audience, audiovisual, audible, audition
credit	believe	credit, discredit, incredible, credulous
dict	speak	predict, contradict, dictate, verdict, diction
duc, duct	lead	conduct, aqueduct, duct, induct, educate
fac	make, do	factory, manufacture, benefactor, facsimile
loc	place	locate, dislocate, relocate, location, allocate
man	hand	manual, manufacture, manuscript, manipulate
migr	move	migrate, immigrant, emigrate, migratory
miss	send	missile, dismiss, missionary, mission, remiss

Latin Roots *(cont.)*

Root	Meaning	Examples
mob	move	automobile, mobile, mobility, mobilize
mot	move	motion, motor, promote, demote, motile
ped	foot	pedal, pedestrian, biped, pedestal
pop	people	population, popular, pop, populace
port	carry	transport, import, portable, porter
rupt	break	erupt, interrupt, rupture, bankrupt, abrupt
sign	mark	signature, signal, significant, insignia
spec	see	inspect, suspect, respect, spectator, spectacle
tract	pull, drag	tractor, subtract, attraction, traction
urb	city	urban, suburb, suburban, urbane
vac	empty	vacant, vacation, vacuum, evacuate, vacate
vid	see	video, evidence, provide, providence

Homophones

add—ad
air—heir
already—all ready
ant—aunt
ate—eight
ball—bawl
bare—bear
be—bee
been—bin
blew—blue
buy—by—bye
cent—sent—scent
clothes—close
creak—creek
dear—deer
die—dye
fair—fare
feet—feat
find—fined
flour—flower
for—four
great—grate
hair—hare
heard—herd
hear—here
hi—high
hole—whole
horse—hoarse
hour—our
in—inn
it's—its
knew—new
lead—led
loan—lone
made—maid
Mary—marry—merry
meat—meet
might—mite
missed—mist
morn—mourn

need—knead
night—knight
no—know
oar—or—ore
one—won
pair—pear
peace—piece
plane—plain
principal—principle
rain—reign—rein
read—red
read—reed
reel—real
right—write
road—rode—rowed
sail—sale
see—sea
seem—seam
sell—cell
shoe—shoo
shone—shown
side—sighed
so—sew—sow
some—sum
steal—steel
sun—son
tail—tale
their—there—they're
threw—through
toe—tow
told—tolled
to—too—two
vary—very
way—weigh
wear—where—ware
weather—whether
week—weak
we—wee—whee
wood—would
your—you're

Important Signs

COLD	KEEP OUT	POISON
DANGER	LADIES	POST OFFICE
DEPOSIT	LOBBY	QUARTER
DOWN	MAIN FLOOR	TAXI
EXIT	MANAGER	TELEPHONE
FIRE ESCAPE	MEN	TICKETS
FREE	NO SMOKING	UP
GAS	NO TRESPASSING	WALK
HOT	OFFICE	WOMEN

Phonics Charts
Easy Consonants

Phonics Chart 1

R ring	**T** top	**N** nut
run red read from our for	to take tell not at it	not no new and in can
S saw	**L** letter	**C** cat
some so see this us yes	little like look will girl school	can come color because second music
D dog	**P** pencil	**M** man
do day down good and said	put pretty page up jump stop	me my mother some from room
B book	**F** fish	**V** valentine
but be boy about remember tub	for from first if before off	very visit voice give leave have

Phonics Charts *(cont.)*
Short Vowels

Phonics Chart 2

A apple	**E** elephant
and at as add can bad man had	end egg every enjoy when get red men
I Indian	**O** octopus
in is it inch with will little did	on off ox October not box stop got

U umbrella

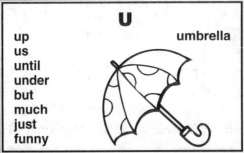

up
us
until
under
but
much
just
funny

1. "E" at the end of a word: The letter "E" is silent at the end of a word.	2. "Y" sounds like long "E" at the end of a word containing another vowel.
are some one like (These vowels are not long. See Chart 5 for the final "E" rule.)	very many any pretty

Phonics Charts *(cont.)*
Difficult Consonants

Phonics Chart 3

	G	girl		**H**	hat
good go get gas again dig big bag			have he had home her him has hit		

	K	king		**W**	window
kind keep kill key like make work book			we with will was away between twenty sandwich		

	J	jar		**QU**	queen
just January jump joy object enjoy major banjo			quite quart quick quack square equal squirrel earthquake		

	X	box		**Y**	yacht		**Z**	zebra
six ax extra Texas box ox tax next			yes you year yellow lawyer canyon			zero zoo zone zipper prize dozen size		

At the end of a short word, say the long "i" sound.

sky	fry
my	why

Phonics Charts *(cont.)*
Consonant Digraphs and Second Sounds

Phonics Chart 4

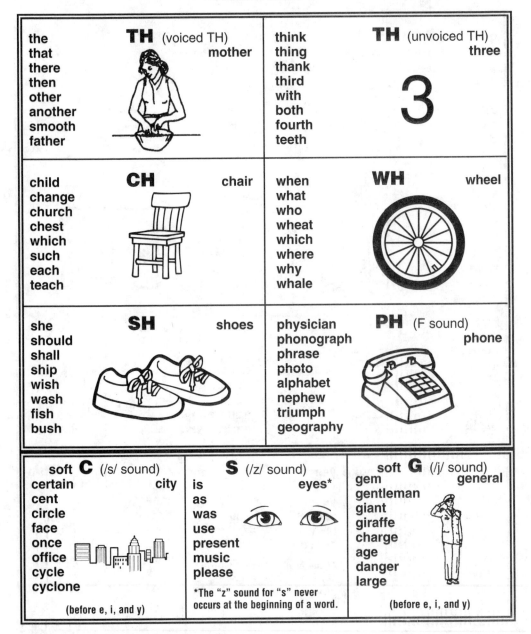

TH (voiced TH) mother	**TH** (unvoiced TH) three
the that there then other another smooth father	think thing thank third with both fourth teeth **3**
CH chair	**WH** wheel
child change church chest which such each teach	when what who wheat which where why whale
SH shoes	**PH** (F sound) phone
she should shall ship wish wash fish bush	physician phonograph phrase photo alphabet nephew triumph geography

soft **C** (/s/ sound) city	**S** (/z/ sound) eyes*	soft **G** (/j/ sound) general
certain cent circle face once office cycle cyclone **(before e, i, and y)**	is as was use present music please *The "z" sound for "s" never occurs at the beginning of a word.	gem gentleman giant giraffe charge age danger large **(before e, i, and y)**

Phonics Charts *(cont.)*
Long Vowels – Final E and Y

Phonics Chart 5

Final "E" Rule: An E at the end of a word frequently makes the vowel long, and the "E" is silent.

a-e		i-e	
make	ate	white	time
take	age	while	fire
came	ace	five	nine
made	able	write	mile
name	ape	ride	like
o-e		**u-e**	
home	alone	use	
those	nose	produce	
close	bone	lube	
hope	pole	pure	
note	rose	tube	

NOTE: Long "E" made by the Final "E" Rule is omitted because of its infrequency.

The Long "E" sound is frequently made by the single letter "Y" at the end of a polysyllabic word (omit digraphs ay and ey).

very	**every**	**country**	**story**
any	**study**	**city**	**carry**

Phonics Charts *(cont.)*
Long Vowels – Open Syllable and Digraphs
Phonics Chart 6

Open Syllable Rule: When a syllable ends in a vowel, that vowel frequently has the long sound.

A	E	I	O	U
A/pril	we	I	so	du/ty
pa/per	be	i/de/a	go	pu/pil
la/dy	he	pi/lot	no	mu/sic
ba/by	e/ven	ti/ny	o/pen	stu/dent
ra/dio		li/on	hell/o	Jan/u/ar/y

Long Vowel Digraphs: There are only six, common, long-vowel digraphs (two letters that make one phoneme).

EA	EE	AI	AY	OA	OW
eat	see	fail	stay	coat	own
year	three	remain	day	soap	know
please	seem	train	gray	road	show
easy	sleep	aid	clay	oak	yellow
sea	tree	chain	crayon	loan	bowl

Phonics Charts *(cont.)*
"Schwa" and Vowel Plus "R"

Phonics Chart 7

SCHWA: The unaccented vowel in a word frequently has the sound of "A" in "ago."

A	E	I	O
about	happen	animal	official
again	problem	office	oppose
away	bulletin	Africa	money
several	hundred	pencil	canyon
China	united	capital	

"ER," "IR," and "UR": These frequently all make the same sound (schwa or short u plus R).

ER	IR	UR
her	first	turn
were	dirt	hurt
other	third	fur
after	sir	hurry
camera	circus	Thursday

"AR" has two sounds:

"AR" as in "far"; "AR" as in "vary"
/air/ sound

"OR" has a unique
/ôr/ sound

AR		OR
/är/	/ar/	/ôr/
star	library	for
are	vary	or
far	Mary	before
start	care	more
hard	January	horn
car	share	

Phonics Charts *(cont.)*
Diphthongs and Other Vowel Sounds

Phonics Chart 8

Broad "O": The /ô/ sound is made by "O," "AL," "AW," and "AU."

O	AL	AW	AU
on	all	draw	because
long	salt	law	author
upon	also	awful	August
off	talk	lawn	haul
song	call	straw	daughter

Diphthongs: They make a sliding sound from one vowel sound to another (one phoneme).

OI	OY	OU	OW
OI and OY make the same sound.		OU and OW make the same sound.	
point	annoy	out	how
voice	enjoy	about	down
noise	toy	our	brown
oil	royal	round	now
boil	oyster	loud	flower

Double "O" and Short "EA"

OO		EA	
Double O		Second sound of EA	
long sound /o͞o/	short sound /o͝o/	Short E sound	
soon	good	dead	
school	foot	ahead	
too	look	heavy	
room	took	ready	
zoo	cook	feather	

Silent Letters

KN		GH	
K before N is silent.		GH is usually silent.	
knife	knot	eight	light
knee	knight	high	right
know	knit	might	caught

Phonics Charts *(cont.)*
Consonant Blends

Phonics Chart 9

R Family

PR—pretty	prince	prize	April
TR—truck	trick	true	extra
GR—grapes	green	grand	hungry
BR—bread	brick	bring	zebra
CR—crab	cry	crow	across
DR—drum	drug	dress	hundred
FR—frog	free	from	afraid

S Family

ST—stamp	stop	stone	best
SP—spoon	sport	spring	crisp
SC—scout	scrub	screw	scoop
SK—skate	sky	skin	mask
SW—swing	swim	sweep	swell
SM—smile	smell	smoke	smart
SN—snow	snake	snap	snooze

L Family

PL—plate	play	please	supply
CL—clock	class	cloud	include
BL—black	blue	blood	tumbler
Fl—flag	flower	fly	snowflake
SL—slow	sleep	sled	asleep
GL—glass	glad	glory	angle

Orphan (no family)

TW—twins	twelve	twice	between

Phonograms

–ab (ă)	–ack (ă)	–ag (ă)	–ail (ā)	–ain (ā)
cab	back	bag	bail	gain
dab	hack	gag	fail	lain
gab	Jack	hag	Gail	main
jab	lack	lag	hail	pain
lab	Mack	rag	jail	rain
nab	pack	sag	mail	vain
tab	quack	tag	nail	brain
blab	rack	wag	pail	chain
crab	sack	brag	quail	drain
drab	black	flag	rail	grain
flab	clack	shag	sail	plain
grab	crack	snag	tail	slain
scab	knack	stag	wail	Spain
slab	shack		frail	sprain
stab	smack		snail	stain
	snack		trail	strain
	stack			train

	–ake (ā)	–am (ă)	–an (ă)	–ank (ă)
	bake	dam	ban	bank
	cake	ham	can	dank
	fake	jam	Dan	Hank
	Jake	Pam	fan	lank
	lake	ram	man	rank
	make	Sam	pan	sank
	quake	tam	ran	tank
	rake	yam	tan	yank
	sake	clam	van	blank
	take	cram	bran	clank
	wake	gram	clan	drank
	brake	scam	flan	flank
	drake	scram	plan	Frank
	flake	sham	scan	plank
	shake	slam	span	prank
	snake	swam	than	shank
		tram		spank
				thank

Phonograms *(cont.)*

–ap (ă)	–at (ă)	–ay (ā)	–ed (ĕ)	–eed (ē)
cap	bat	bay	bed	deed
gap	cat	day	fed	feed
lap	fat	gay	led	heed
map	gnat	hay	Ned	need
nap	hat	jay	red	reed
rap	mat	lay	Ted	seed
sap	pat	may	wed	weed
tap	rat	pay	bled	bleed
clap	sat	ray	bred	breed
flap	tat	say	fled	creed
scrap	vat	clay	Fred	freed
slap	brat	gray	shed	greed
snap	chat	play	shred	speed
strap	drat	pray	sled	steed
trap	flat	spray	sped	treed
	scat	stay		
	slat	tray		
	spat			

	–ell (ĕ)	–est (ĕ)	–ew (ĕ)	–ick (ĭ)
	bell	best	dew	Dick
	cell	jest	few	kick
	dell	nest	hew	lick
	fell	pest	Jew	Nick
	hell	rest	knew	pick
	jell	test	pew	quick
	Nell	vest	blew	Rick
	sell	west	brew	sick
	tell	zest	chew	tick
	well	blest	drew	wick
	yell	chest	flew	brick
	dwell	crest	screw	chick
	quell	quest	skew	click
	shell		slew	flick
	smell			slick

Phonograms *(cont.)*

–ight (ī)	–ill (ĭ)	–im (ĭ)	–in (ĭ)	–ine (ī)
fight	bill	dim	bin	dine
knight	dill	him	din	fine
light	fill	Jim	fin	line
might	gill	Kim	gin	mine
night	hill	rim	kin	nine
right	Jill	Tim	pin	pine
sight	kill	brim	sin	tine
tight	mill	grim	tin	vine
blight	pill	prim	win	wine
bright	quill	slim	chin	brine
flight	sill	swim	grin	shine
fright	till	trim	shin	shrine
plight	will	whim	skin	spine
slight	chill		spin	swine
	drill		thin	whine
	spill		twin	
	still			
	thrill			

	–ing (ĭ)	–ink (ĭ)	–ip (ĭ)	–ob (ŏ)
	bing	kink	dip	Bob
	ding	link	hip	cob
	king	mink	lip	fob
	ping	pink	nip	gob
	ring	rink	rip	job
	sing	sink	sip	knob
	wing	wink	tip	lob
	zing	blink	chip	mob
	bring	brink	clip	rob
	cling	chink	drip	sob
	fling	clink	flip	blob
	sling	drink	grip	slob
	spring	shrink	ship	snob
	sting	stink	skip	
	string	think	slip	
	swing		strip	
			trip	
			whip	

Phonograms *(cont.)*

–ock (ŏ)	–op (ŏ)	–ore (ŏ)	–ot (ŏ)
dock	bop	bore	cot
hock	cop	core	got
knock	hop	fore	hot
lock	mop	gore	jot
mock	pop	more	knot
rock	sop	pore	lot
sock	top	sore	not
tock	chop	tore	pot
block	crop	wore	rot
clock	drop	score	tot
crock	flop	shore	blot
flock	plop	spore	clot
frock	prop	store	plot
shock	shop	swore	shot
smock	slop		slot
stock	stop		spot

–out (ou)	–ow (ou)	–ug (ŭ)	–unk (ŭ)	–y (ī)
bout	bow	bug	bunk	by
gout	cow	dug	dunk	my
out	how	hug	funk	cry
pout	now	jug	hunk	dry
rout	row	lug	junk	fly
tout	sow	mug	punk	fry
clout	vow	pug	sunk	ply
flout	brow	rug	chunk	pry
grout	chow	tug	drunk	shy
scout	plow	chug	flunk	sky
shout	prow	drug	plunk	sly
snout		plug	shrunk	spy
spout		shrug	skunk	try
sprout		slug	spunk	why
stout		smug	stunk	
trout			trunk	

Phonics Survey Test: Directions

Phonics is an important and useful skill associated with reading. Poor ability in phonics does not always mean poor reading ability, but if reading ability is poor, it can often be aided by having phonics instructions.

How to Test

Use the test at the bottom of the page. Ask the student to read the nonsense words aloud. Tell him or her that these are not real words. If he or she makes an error, allow a second chance (but not a third).

How to Score

Using a copy of the record sheet on page 139, mark each word that is read incorrectly. On the right-hand side, note whether the student was "perfect," "knew some," or "knew none" for each of the following skills: consonants, short vowels, long vowels, difficult vowels. (The "Charts" referred to in parentheses are the Phonics Charts on page 125-133.) This information will be very useful in selection materials for phonics instruction.

Phonics Survey: Student Copy				
Directions: Read each line of nonsense words.				
Section 1				
TIF	NEL	ROM		
DUP	CAV	SEB		
Section 2				
KO	HOAB	WAJE	KE	YATE
ZEEX	QUIDE	YAIG	ZAY	SUDE
Sections 3				
WHAW	THOIM	PHER	KOYCH	
OUSH	CHAU	EANG	HOON	

Phonics Survey Test

This survey gives a general idea of the number of phonics skills that the student knows.

Name _____

Examiner _____ Date _____

Directions:

1. The student reads each line of nonsense words using phonics rules.

2. The teacher checks the box to right of the line, according to the number known.

NOTE: This survey may be repeated at a later date after more phonics instruction, or the teacher can make up nonsense words for testing or instruction.

						Perfect	Knew Some	Knew None
Section 1—Easy Consonants and Short Vowels (Charts 1 and 2)								
TIF	NEL	ROM				☐	☐	☐
DUP	CAV	SEB				☐	☐	☐
Section 2—Difficult Consonants and Long Vowels (Charts 3, 5, and 6)								
KO	HOAB	WAJE	KE	YATE		☐	☐	☐
ZEEX	QUIDE	YAIG	ZAY	SUDE		☐	☐	☐
Sections 3—Consonant Digraphs and Difficult Vowels (Charts 4, 7, and 8)								
WHAW	THOIM	PHER	KOYCH			☐	☐	☐
OUSH	CHAU	EANG	HOON			☐	☐	☐

Story Starters List

Use the following suggestions as story titles or opening sentences. Also, see the interest inventories on pages 92 and 93 for story starter suggestions.

- **I often remember . . .**
- **If I were a cloud . . .**
- **My family . . .**
- **I never . . .**
- **The best vacation . . .**
- **A barking dog means . . .**
- **What would happen if . . .**
- **Accidents are caused by . . .**
- **Once I got lost . . .**
- **People think that I . . .**
- **The biggest problem in the world is . . .**
- **The latest fashion . . .**
- **I get mad when. . .**
- **The farthest away from home I've been . . .**
- **I dream about . . .**
- **The phone rang at 3 A.M. . . .**
- **Ants think about . . .**
- **I want to know more about . . .**
- **Just for fun we could. . .**
- **The most beautiful thing I ever saw . . .**
- **Rain always . . .**

Handwriting Charts

Additional Instructional Materials

The following materials by Dr. Fry are published by Teacher Created Materials and available at most school supply stores.

Assessment and Comprehension

Informal Reading Assessments— TCM3074

Nonfiction Comprehension Test Practice:

    Level 2—TCM3509

    Level 3—TCM3510

    Level 4—TCM3511

    Level 5—TCM3512

    Level 6—TCM3513

Pocket Charts—TCM3522

Pre-Phonics Tests—TCM2667

Instant Words

1000 Instant Words—TCM2757

Instant Word Practice Book— TCM3503

Instant Words Bingo—TCM3523

Instant Words Flashcards Set A— TCM2661

Instant Words Flashcards Set B— TCM2662

Picture Nouns—TCM2763

Picture Nouns Flashcards Set A— TCM2665

Picture Nouns Flashcards Set B— TCM3501

Phonics

Phonics Charts—TCM2762

Phonics Flashcards Set A— TCM2663

Phonics Flashcards Set B— TCM3502

Phonics Patterns—TCM2761

Phonogram Flashcards—TCM2664

Word Charts:

  Blends and Digraphs—TCM3504

  Long Vowels—TCM1769

  Mixed Vowels—TCM3506

  Short Vowels—TCM1796

  Vowel Combinations—TCM3505

  All five charts—TCM6641

Spelling and Writing

Alphabet Flashcards—TCM2666

Beginning Writer's Manual— TCM2759

Computer Keyboarding—TCM2764

Homophones Workbook—TCM2668

Spelling Book: Grades 1-6— TCM2750

Spelling Checkers—TCM2699

Vocabulary Fun—TCM2765

Word Book—TCM2758

Index

Alphabet, 60, 61, 141

Basal readers, 26

Bilingual, 39

Bingo game, 50, 51, 65, 66

Book lists, 94, 95

Character traits, 36

Children's literature, 26, 27

Cloze, 38

Comparison, 37

Comprehension, 11, 30–41, 80

Concentration game, 53

Conclusions, 36

Consonant charts, 62, 125, 127, 128, 133

Discipline, 17

Experience charts, 72, 73

Expository writing, 76

Flash cards, 48-50, 108, 116

Fluency, 19, 21, 30, 31, 80

Frustration reading level, 10, 21, 88-91

Games, 50-53

Handwriting, 74-76

    Charts, 141

Homophones, 58, 123

Idiomatic expressions, 42

Independent reading level, 10, 21, 88-91

Informal matching, 10, 23

Instant Words, 13, 14, 46, 47, 108-113

Instructional materials, 142

Instructional reading level, 10, 21, 88-91

Interest, 17

Interest Inventory, 25

    For Children, 92

    For Adults, 93

Jokes, 28

Language experience approach, 70, 71

Leveling, 23

Listening, 77, 78

Long answers, 38

Love, 16

Main idea, 36

Matching, 10, 22, 23

Multiple-choice questions, 38

Oral Reading Test, 9, 20, 21, 82-91

Pairs game, 51-53

Phoneme awareness, 61-63

Phonics, 14, 15, 63-68, 125-133

    Charts, 64, 65, 125-133

    Diagnosing, 64

    Methods of teaching, 64-67

    Place of teaching, 59, 60

    Survey Test, 138, 139

    Warning, 68

Phonograms, 67, 68, 134-137

Picture Nouns, 54, 55, 116, 117

Predictable Story, 27

Prefixes, 56, 118, 119

Index *(cont.)*

Questions
  5 W's + H, 37
  Multiple-choice, 38
  Student-generated, 39
  Types of, 34-37
  Variety, 34–37
Readability graph, 10, 24
Reading:
  Ability (determining), 9, 20
  Comprehension, 11, 30
  Definitions, 7–8
  Ideas, 79, 80
  Levels, 10, 21, 88-91
  Materials, 10, 22-29, 94, 95
  Numbers, 29
  Practice, 47, 48
Repetitious story, 27
Retelling, 39
Rewards, 18
Rime, 68
Roots, 56
  Greek, 120
  Latin, 121, 122
Setting, 35
Short Answers, 38
Sign words, 29, 124
Silent Reading Comprehension Test, 41, 96-107
Songs, 43
Speaking, 76, 77, 79

Special/unconventional reading material, 27
Spelling, 53, 54, 66, 67
Story starters, 71, 140
Student-written stories, 73, 74
Subject matter variety, 31, 32
Success, 16
Summary, 35
Tests:
  Instant Words, 45, 114, 115
  Oral Reading, 82-91
  Phonics Survey, 138, 139
  Silent Reading Comprehension, 41, 96-107
  Standardized Silent Reading, 40
Time sequence, 35
Trade secrets, 16-19
Variety:
  Difficulty of level of material, 37
  Length of reading selection, 32-34
  Response, 38
  Subject matter, 31, 32
Types of questions, 34-37
Vocabulary:
  Basic sight, 44, 46
  Building, 33, 56, 57
Vowel charts, 126, 129-132,
Word study method, 54
Writing, 15, 60, 61, 69
  Expository, 76